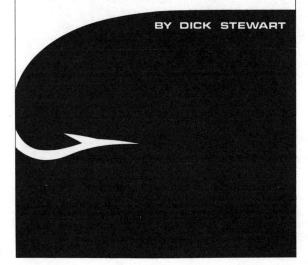

the Hook Book

A REFERENCE GUIDE FOR FLY TYERS

BY DICK STEWART

Northland Press, Inc.
Intervale, NH

Other books by Dick Stewart:

Universal Fly Tying Guide
Trolling Flies for Trout and Salmon (with Bob Leeman)

Published by Northland Press, Inc.
P.O. Box 280
Intervale, N.H. 03860
USA

Cover design by Larry Largay

Second Edition

ISBN 0-936644-02-8

Contents

From Stone to Steel   7

Nomenclature   11

Future Fly Hooks   14

Measurement Procedures   17

Hook Pages:

     Eagle Claw   24 to 31

     Kamasan   32 to 34

     Mustad   35 to 60

     Partridge   61 to 80

     Tiemco   81 to 87

     VMC   88 to 95

Acknowledgements

This book could not have possibly been created without the extensive help of many other people who deserve substantial appreciation. First to my partner, Fred Abbruzzese, who helped provide me the time to undertake such a project. Thanks, also, to Mark Barlow, Eric Brown and Bill Franke who assisted in every step along the way and who spent many hours pouring over hooks, taking measurements, and providing encouragement.

To the hook manufacturers and their distributors: specifically Wright and McGill, producers of Eagle Claw; Worldwide Importers, distributors of Kamasan; Mustad USA; Umpqua Feather Merchants, importers of Tiemco; and VMC, I would like to recognize their donation of hooks and information. A special thanks to Alan Bramley, Managing Director of Partridge of Redditch, for not only his generous sharing of information, but for also making it possible for me to have a first hand tour of their hookmaking facility in England.

Thanks to my son, Bob, who helped pave the way for me to learn enough about computers to be willing to undertake this project, and lastly a warm thanks to my wife Kathy, who may forever be finding hooks and feathers in our carpet at home.

October 1986

Introduction

This is a book intended for those of us who enjoy the pastime of tying our own fishing flies. Through these pages I will describe and illustrate most of the hooks designed for, or suitable to be used in, fly tying applications. Whether for trout, salmon, steelhead, bass, bluefish, tarpon or bonefish - all are represented here. Traditional hooks are complemented with special purpose fly hooks.

Novice fly tyers will learn about hook construction, design, nomenclature, and application. More experienced tyers will be most interested in having a single reference source, together with the technical information which will permit a comparison of different hooks. Possibly, and hopefully, manufacturers will reconsider their personal preferences and view fly tying hooks as a special category in need of greater standardization.

We fly tyers have many advantages over the non-fly tying anglers. Not only can we have more flies at streamside; not only do we have an enhanced ability to experiment; not only do we learn more about the food forms these flies represent; not only do we receive satisfaction from the results of our handywork - but we're able to extend the pleasures of our fishing season throughout the year. It would be difficult to total all the fish caught in my imagination as I've sat at my fly tying vise over the years. Perhaps the pages of this book will add a bit to the pursuit of imaginary fish, and possibly to the landing of the real ones.

Although I have provided a brief background of hookmaking, it is not my intention to elaborate in this respect. Anyone interested in pursuing this aspect of hooks should refer to the available literature, and I would recommend the books listed in the bibliography.

The extensive statistical data contained in the "Hook Pages" has been gathered with the upmost attention paid to providing accuracy. I have no desire to praise or fault any particular manufacturer, but simply to provide the data for the benefit of fly tyers everywhere.

FROM STONE TO STEEL

Archaeologists have uncovered fish hooks dating back some 7,000 years to the Stone Age and it is believed likely that wood, bone or horn hooks might have pre-dated the stone remains. Copper, bronze and then iron hooks track the evolution of hook development and examples of these early works are housed in museums today. As historians seek to uncover the earliest references to "fly fishing" it would appear that the use of the artificial "fly" or "lure" may have been even earlier than had been thought previously.

Sometime toward the end of the Middle Ages hookmaking is assumed to have become a specialized craft, and during the fifteenth century a description of making hooks (from needles) appears in *The Boke of St. Albans,* possibly written by Dame Juliana Berners. The earliest reference to hookmaking as a trade is found in Isaac Walton's *The Compleat Angler* in 1653, in which he refers to Charles Kirby in London as "the most exact and best hook-maker this nation affords".

It was in Britain where hookmaking first developed as part of the industrial revolution. Hookmaking was spread out geographically in places such as Dublin and Limerick, Ireland; Aberdeen, Scotland; and Carlisle, England - names associated with hook shapes today. The town of Redditch, near Birmingham, was located in an inland district which became a center for fine steel and wire. This area evolved as a major producer of needles and by the mid-1800's a number of hookmakers had appeared. It was from this district, and specifically from Redditch, that many other names, familiar to this day, were associated with hookmaking. Names like Bartleet, Alcock, Sealey, and Milward. Also from England we have inherited names from Mr. Kirby and Mr. Sproat, both early hook designers.

Shortly following the British advances in hookmaking, the Norwegian hook industry had it's start when Sheriff Ole Mustad, and his son Hans, began hook production. From these beginnings in 1876, O. Mustad & Son has grown to become the worlds largest hook producer.

Despite the growth of hookmaking elsewhere, England continued to dominate in the production of fly tying hooks. As fly tyers, our roots all extend back to England. The fly dressings, the techniques and the materials used all have a British heritage - so, too, the hooks. The finest craftsmen continued hook production into the twentieth century and until interrupted by World War II, their firms continued to satisfy the demands for quality fly tying hooks.

Today only one major English producer of the fly tying hooks continues, A. E. Partridge & Son, who absorbed the remains of some of it's notable predecessors. They still concentrate on specialized hooks for the fly tying industry, maintaining that tradition for which England is highly regarded.

The manufacturing of fishing hooks has become mechanized, and in some instances fully automated, utilizing very complex machinery. The essential hookmaking procedure begins with the use of wire, usually a high carbon content steel. Occasionally steel alloys are also used. Once a wire of a proper diameter has been selected, it is cut to the exact predetermined length that will be required for a finished hook of a particular size and style. The next step is to "point" the wire. While in the past the points were hand-filed by experienced craftsmen, today they are either shaped on a grinding machine or else they are cut on the diagonal to form a point. Following the pointing process, if a tapered eye is specified in the hook design then the forward end of the wire is ground to the appropriate taper.

The next requirement is to create the hook's barb which is accomplished by cutting into the wire at an acute angle and raising a small sliver of metal resulting in a barb. Here, too, the depth of the slice must be extremely precise since too deep a cut would substantially reduce the hook's strength.

"Shaping" the hook, or forming a bend, is next achieved by physically bending the wire to conform to the shape of an established form. Toolmakers create forms to the size and shape of individual hook styles, and must make a form for each hook size within a style. These resulting dies exactly match the inside radius of the hook shape desired. With the wire point and barb firmly held in position, the wire is then forced to wrap, or bend, around the selected die. The result of this procedure is a wire incorporating the desired shape of the bend. The die configuration determines whether the shape is a Sproat, Kirby, Limerick, etc.

Forging is a term applied to a process of forming metal. In hookmaking it refers to the flattening of the round wire in such a manner as to increase its strength in one plane, or direction. Commonly, hooks are forged on both sides beginning at a point behind the barb, and extending throughout the bend up to the hook shank. Often the forging will include much of the hook shank as well. By flattening both sides of the hook, the strength along a theoretical straight line of pull is increased. The process of forging is accomplished by simply placing individual hooks into a press which flattens the round wire to a controlled thickness.

The last stage of forming the typical fly tying hook is the creation of the "eye". Again the procedure involves bending the foreward end of the wire around a form of the appropriate diameter. The form in this instance is simply a metal peg. The hook is held stationary while the foreward end of the wire is wrapped around this peg. This seems a simple enough process when one envisions large hook eyes being formed, but for the tiny dry fly hooks it might be remembered that this peg is smaller in thickness than your 3X tippet material. A final bend of the hook wire may now be made if the eye is to be 'turned up" or "turned down".

"Chemical sharpening" is a term which has only recently been used in connection with hookmaking. It refers to a rather simple process whereby hooks, once completely formed, are immersed into an acid bath which dissolves any minute burrs or abrasions which occured during manufacture. The result, under proper controls, is a cleaner metal surface and, thus, sharper hooks. An increased number of hook producers are now now utilizing this technique although they may refer to it by different terms than the name chemical sharpening.

The soft carbon steel wire must now be hardened to achieve an improved strength. This is accomplished by tempering the metal. Hooks are placed in an oven which heats them throughout, and they are then immersed in a liquid coolant, often a closely guarded secret formula, which brings about a rapid decrease in temperature. This process hardens the metal, significantly increasing its resistance to bending.

The next stage of the production flow is to clean the metal in preparation of receiving its final protective coating. There are various means used but they are represented by the tumbling process whereby the hooks are cleaned with an abrasive.

Applying the hook's finish is the last step before a final inspection and packaging. Most all of the common fly tying hooks have a finish described as "bronze". This simply refers to the approximate color of the hook which results from applying one or more coats of clear, or amber hued, lacquer to the hooks surface. Trays of hooks are coated with lacquer, they are then heated or baked in ovens, and a second coat is often applied and the process repeated. Black finishes, sometimes referred to as "Japanned Black", are simply a pigmented lacquer used in the same manner. Almost any color can be applied at this stage but bronze and black have been those colors used most traditionally by fly tyers. Silver and gold finishes can, optionally, be used. Here the finish is achieved by electroplating rather than by lacquering.

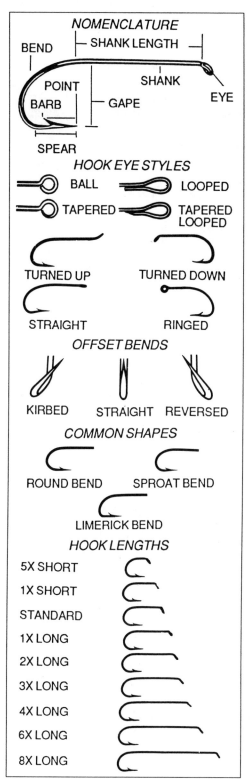

NOMENCLATURE

NOMENCLATURE
- SHANK LENGTH
- BEND
- POINT
- SHANK
- EYE
- BARB
- GAPE
- SPEAR

HOOK EYE STYLES
- BALL
- LOOPED
- TAPERED
- TAPERED LOOPED

TURNED UP   TURNED DOWN

STRAIGHT   RINGED

OFFSET BENDS
- KIRBED   STRAIGHT   REVERSED

COMMON SHAPES
- ROUND BEND   SPROAT BEND
- LIMERICK BEND

HOOK LENGTHS
- 5X SHORT
- 1X SHORT
- STANDARD
- 1X LONG
- 2X LONG
- 3X LONG
- 4X LONG
- 6X LONG
- 8X LONG

NOMENCLATURE

Despite proposals which have appeared over many decades, the hook making industry has made little progress in arriving at any standard on which fly tyers may rely. For example, between different manufacturers hook sizes are often determined by differing proprietary standards. One producers standard size 14 hook may have a gape equal to another company's standard size 18 hook. Shank lengths also vary, while descriptions of wire weight and shape of bend often serve only to confuse the buyer. Commentators, like Alan Bramley of Partridge Hooks, have proposed the adoption of a hook standard. Datus Proper, author of *What the Trout Said*, has clearly demonstrated inconsistencies in hook descriptions, and has also called for some reform to bring about a standard.

My own experience in this area has led me to agree with these writers. However, the manufacturers lack of interest in a cooperative effort has suggested a different approach--perhaps we could begin by agreeing on the terminology of fly tying hooks. Moreover, perhaps we, the fly tying community, could help set this standard. If fly tyers, authors, dealers and instructors might agree on a hook nomenclature, it might serve as a first step toward standardization.

GAPE OR GAP

There is no confusion here about the measurement, which is the shortest distance between the hook point and hook shank. Among the hook producers, those located in English speaking countries have traditionally used Gape whereas the term Gap is used exclusively by manufacturers in countries whose language is other than English. Here we would suggest that the use of Gape be adopted by English language writers.

SHAPE OR BEND

Both terms have been utilized to describe a hook's particular curvature. With respectful deference to J. Edson Leonard, whose book *Flies* served as my earliest instruction, it seems to me more proper to use the term Bend as a noun referring to the specific part of the hook, and to use the term Shape as a descriptive adjective. Thus, we would refer to the "shape of the bend". A "sproat" bend or "limerick" bend, where both sproat and limerick are shapes used to describe the Shape of the Bend.

OFFSET BENDS

If the point of a hook is not in the same plane as the shank, i.e., if it is bent to one side, it is termed as Offset, as opposed to straight. The terms "kirbed" or "reversed" further signify whether the point is offset to the right or left side. Some manufacturers simply state "offset" in describing their hooks, while others give us a more complete description. While hooks with offset bends are used only infrequently in fly tying, I can think of no reason not to use the full description.

SHANK LENGTH

Has traditionally signified the measurement from behind the hook eye to that point where the hook begins to curve. Although it has been suggested that this measurement might be called "body length", and it's also been argued that the measurement might extend to include the eye, these ideas have gathered only limited support. My tendency is to favor the more traditional "shank length" as the descriptive standard. Manufacturers often designate hook shank length as being 1X, or 2X, or 3X long (or short). This terminology means that the hook is longer than the "standard" shank length for the same style hook. A 2X long shank is equal in length to the shank of the standard hook which is two sizes larger. For example, a size 12 hook, 2X long, has a hook shank length equal to the same style "standard" hook in a size 10. Notice that for purposes of this length designation, it is assumed that hook sizes change in increments of one. To further complicate matters, not all hook producers adhere to this formula, and inconsistencies abound.

POINT AND SPEAR

The term point describes both the sharp tip end of a hook as well as the entire portion ranging from that tip to the hook barb. Spear, on the other hand, represents that portion of the hook measured from the bottom of the bend, foreward to the tip of the point. I don't see any way to avoid the confusion resulting from using the term point in it's dual role.

THROAT

Is the distance from the front end of the hook point to the furthest depth of the bend. If this distance is too short it is agreed that there is a greater chance that a fish might free itself from the hook.

HEEL

Is customarily used to refer to that portion of the bend which is affected by the forging process.

EYE

Represents the forward part of the hook, to which the fishing line or leader is attached. Modern hooks are either ball (sometimes called "ringed", a confusing designation as you will soon note) or looped, and are either tapered or untapered. The finished eye is either straight, or is turned up or turned down. On a very few hook models the eye is turned 90 degrees to a position in the same plane as the hook bend. This style eye is termed "ringed".

FUTURE FLY HOOKS

The past 20 years or so have brought about a great deal of change in all aspects of fly fishing, and fly tying in particular. We've witnessed increased participation in our pasttime, and the utilization and introduction of many new fly tying materials and techniques. Perhaps the differences in hook design have not been as notable as advances in rods, reels, flylines and such but such change is evolving and I would suspect that we've seen only the bare beginnings.

Other influences have occurred which might impact on future hook design. There is a firm tendency toward more exact imitation of the food forms we represent with our flies. Obviously one of the greatest barriers to achieving realism is the hook itself. The tyer will continue to try to minimize the hooks interference with their goal of imitating nature. They will stretch the limits by using lighter and finer wire hooks. The result will be either more extended body flys or the use of long shank hooks in smaller sizes. Either choice will place great demands on a hook's strength. The greatly increased strength of modern leader and tippet materials, which will no longer break before the hook fails, will only exaggerate the consideration of the hook's bend resistance.

An increase in "catch-and-release" fisheries will be accompanied by a growing interest in barbless, or near barbless, hooks. As anglers learn they can live without, and possibly even be more successful with, a minimum barb configuration, they will be seeking hooks which meet that standard. I personally think a "mini barb" would result in the greatest commercial success as totally barbless hooks have failed to encounter broad public acceptance.

The new leader materials with their greatly increased strength for smaller diameters tend to make the large hook eye redundant. I would suspect that on larger fly tying hooks the manufacturers might consider reducing the size of the hook eye.

At the risk of being pretentious, I would like to speculate, on future considerations in hook design. The pages of this book suggest a first step which is not in the hook itself, but rather in their presentation to the buyer. We've long lived with standards that are both confusing and non-informative. The sizing of hooks is a primary example. Simply stated, there is only limited uniformity among manufacturers, and even individual producers don't adhere well to a single standard. Not gape, not length, not weight, not shape, not strength - none of these are uniformly presented to the consumer. While I believe that the closest we come to a concensus is in using gape as the starting point, I would suggest that we'll begin to see more attention paid to these specifics and that future packaging will give use more meaningful information.

The "shorty" fly fishing vest was designed to allow the angler to wade deeper in the water without soaking the contents of his pockets. To alleviate this problem I purchased a shorty vest and soon discovered it merely meant I was in deeper water when everything got wet. Now at the end of a days fishing I always seem to have priorities other than meticulously emptying my vest and fully drying its contents. Over the course of a season the net result is a handful of rusting hooks. My light Cahills turn amber and I can no longer distinguish those Comparadun colors I so carefully scrutinized at my tying bench. I've also lost more than one good fish due to hook failure resulting from undetected rust. Probably the fear of increased cost has been a major consideration in the failure to introduce rustless hooks, but if we consider the hook as representing perhaps only 5 to 10 percent of the finished flys value, it simply doesn't make sense. I'd much rather pay extra for hooks but be assured that rust wouldn't plague my fly box. Advances in metallurgy and chemistry have provided us the technology to produce rust resistant hooks; it's time to produce them for fly tyers.

Hook color, too, has been an annoyance to my understanding of fly tying. Somehow it seems inconsistent that we tie both a Black Gnat and a White Miller, both on an almost black hook. Once wet the fly will often discolor; light colored flies becoming darker, revealing the underlying hook color. This observation is certainly not unique to me as respected authors have suggested a variety of ways to avoid this problem as we tie our flies. The nagging question remains, however, why are almost all fly tying hooks bronze? I would like to experiment with silver finished hooks for dry flies and emerging nymphs. Would the protruding hook shank be less conspicuous than bronze? Might it reflect it's surroundings? Might it better resemble the discarded nymphal shuck? I doubt that it would add significantly to hook costs to offer silver, as well as darker hooks. Let's hope we get to try some.

As interest in flyfishing for bass and saltwater species explodes, tyers have been forced to use hooks designed for other purposes on which to tie their flies. With the exception of the "Stinger Hook" (Mustad # 37186) no new hooks have been offered for these markets. Bass fishermen need hooks with a strength which will permit them to "cross the eyes" of bass when setting the hooks, and the larger bass flies present unique fly tying challenges for which existing hooks are not expressly designed. I anticipate we'll see some specialty bass hooks within the next few years. The saltwater fly fisherman requires greater strength and sharpness in lighter wire hooks. With corrosion resistance an essential demand I would expect to witness the use of either exotic metals such as titanium, or else a product of modern chemistry bonded to high strength alloys.

Plastic fishhooks? There has been some investigation in their direction but we haven't yet seen the technology advance to the point where it would be of interest to fly fishermen, but then years ago many of us didn't forsee carbon graphite either.

Overall, I anticipate that the next ten years we will produce more positive change in fly tying hooks. With continued growth in fly fishing, with increased catch and release fishing, we'll see smaller hook barbs. Hooks will increasingly be produced to meet the specialized needs of fly tyers - and these tyers will be willing to pay higher prices. After all, who would have thought we would pay today's high prices for quality dry fly necks or finely machined fly tying vises.

TESTING
PROCEDURES

On the following descriptive "Hook Pages" I have presented the important hooks that are being used in fly tying. Almost any hook can be used to tie some sort of fly and we are not concerned with these exceptions here, but rather to present the fly tyer with a reference to these fly hooks they are most likely to consider. The pages are divided first into sections in alphabetical order based on manufacturer's trade name. Within each brand the hooks are listed in alphabetical or numerical order. There are a few instances in which fishing tackle retailers have these same hooks packaged under their own individual trade name, or may have a custom hook fabricated which is not generally available through other distributors. These, too, were excluded from consideration.

The descriptive information about each hook style, i.e. wire, shape, eye, length, finish and size range, was taken from the manufacturer's catalogs and price lists, and was based on availability in the United States. In some instances other hooks and sizes are also being produced but are not readily available in this country.

I have attempted to provide suggestions as to how a hook might be commonly used. Of course anyone can select a hook to meet their particular design and a hook I suggest be used for dry flies might also be the perfect selection for a light wire wet fly.

The substitution possibilities listed represent those hook models and styles that might be used in place of the subject hook. The substitutes listed are those models which have design characteristics, of shape, length and strength which might be interchangable.

The "Specifications" section is intended to establish a more precise comparison among hooks. Metric standards were used for all data because they provides more meaningful comparison.

The exception to this is "bend resistance" where ounces served as the measuring unit. We thought it might be the most meaningful reference for the reader. Measurements were performed in the following manner:

Measuring length

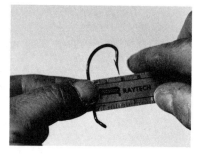

Measuring gape

Shank Length: Measured from a point immediately behind the hook eye to the beginning of the bend. Essentially , this represents the usable length of the hook shank unless the fly tyer extends the body into the curved portion of the wire. Knowing this measurement is of particular importance when imitating insects with a very specific body length.

Gape: Is the distance between the point and the hook shank. While it has been customarily accepted that there is a relatively standard relationship between gape and hook size, a review of the actual measurements will reveal this is not necessarily true. At the extreme we found gapes of 4 mm. on hooks which were sized all the way from #10 to #18.

Weight: Was calculated using a sensitive jeweler's balance, weighing ten or more hooks at a time, and establishing the average weight. Of interest might be the minimal weight differences between some standard "wet fly" and "dry fly" hooks.

Wire Diameter: Measurements were taken on the round unforged portion of the hook wire using a blade micrometer. Because of rounding errors, measurements may vary ±.03 mm.

Measuring wire diameter

Weighing hooks

18

Bend Resistance: It was desired to establish some measure of each hooks strength, relative to other hooks. Following much consideration we elected to take what amounted to a conservative approach. We decided that the greatest opportunity for hook failure was when the point was subject to maximum leverage, and that the risk of "practical failure" was likely to occur when the hook point moved 60 degrees from it's original position, or if it broke prior to attaining 60 degrees. To make such measurements we made a hook-holding device of aluminum stock and affixed it to a metalworking lathe bed which would permit the application of steady, gradual pressure.

Device for testing bend resistance

The hook was positioned so that the tip of the point remained stationary as force was applied through a wire inserted in the hook eye. Behind the hook an adjustable plate permitted us to align the natural hook point with a line, (our zero line) and this plate also contained a mark 60 degrees from zero so that we could visibly determine our theoretical point of failure. As force was applied a scale permitted a reading "bend resistance" or the number of ounces of force required to bend the hook to 60 degrees.

Hook before bending   Hook bent to 60°

Two scales were employed; one used for larger hooks measured in 2 ounce increments while a second provided more accurate one ounce increments for smaller hooks. Two hooks of each size

19

were tested and the results were accepted if both hooks provided identical scale readings. Up to five more hooks were tested if we found any variance in the original two measurements. While a close look at the tables provided on the Hook Pages will reveal an overall consistancy of results, some anomalies occurred and we can only assure the reader of our testing accuracy. It should be emphasized that the absolute figures, i.e. the exact number of ounces of bend resistance, is probably not a very meaningful figure. It is an extreme measure of an arbitrary point of failure.

On the other hand, strength can be a critical consideration in hook selection, and a comparison between sizes, models, or brands is bound to generate some interest. Knowing that one hook has twice the bend resistance of another might well influence the fly tyers choice.

Bibliography

Fly Tyer Magazine,
 Whitlock, Dave;   Vol. 1, Issue 2
 --------   Vol. 1, Issue 3
 Fenner, J.E.;   Vol. 5, Issue 3
 Proper, Datus C.;   Vol. 6, Issue 3
 --------   Vol. 6, Issue 4
 --------   Vol. 7, Issue 1
 Stewart, Dick;   Vol. 8, Issue 4

Herter, George Leonard; *Professional Fly Tying and Tackle Making Manuel,* Brown Publishing Company, Waseca, MN, 1953

Hurum, Hans Jorgen; *A History of the Fish Hook,* A & C Black, Ltd., London, 1977

Leonard, J. Edson; *Flies,* A.S. Barnes and Co., Inc., New York, 1950

McClane, A.J. (ed.); *McClane's Standard Fishing Encyclopedia,* Holt Rinehart and Winston, New York, 1965

Proper, Datus C.; *What the Trout Said,* Alfred A. Knopf, New York 1982

U.S.A. Hook Distributors

Eagle Claw
>Wright & McGill
>P.O. Box 16011
>Denver, CO 80216

Kamasan
>World Wide Outfitters
>425 College Ave.
>Santa Rosa, CA 95401

Mustad
>O. Mustad & Son (USA) Inc.
>P.O. Box 838
>Auburn, NY 13021

Partridge
>Partridge (USA)
>P.O. Box 585
>Wakefield, MA 01880

Tiemco
>Umpqua Feather Merchants
>P.O. Box 700
>Glide, OR 97443

VMC
>VMC, Inc.
>1901 Oakcrest Ave.
>St. Paul, MN 55113

HOOK PAGES

(all hooks are illustrated at actual size)

57

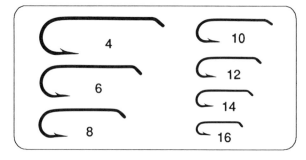

Wire: Regular
Shape: Sproat
Eye: Ball, turned down
Finish: Bronze
Sizes: 4 to 16

Common Uses: Wet flies and nymphs.

Possible Substitutes: Kamasan B-170; Mustad 3906; Partridge G3A; VMC 8527

Specifications:

SIZES:	4	6	8	10	12	14	16
Shank Length (mm)	17	14	12	10	9	7	6
Gape (mm)	9	8	6	5.5	4	3	2.5
Weight (grams)	205	190	87	66	45	31	23
Wire Diameter (mm)	.89	.81	.69	.63	.61	.53	.48
Bend Resistance (oz.)	74	38	34	30	32	26	24

58

Wire: Regular
Shape: Round
Eye: Ball, turned down
Finish: Bronze
Sizes: 4 to 16

Common Uses: Streamers, bucktails, stonefly nymphs and muddlers.

Possible Substitutes: Mustad 9672; Partridge D4A; Tiemco TMC 5263

Specifications:

SIZES:	4	6	8	10	12	14	16
Shank Length (mm)	26	21	17	15	13	12	10
Gape (mm)	9	7.5	6.5	6	5	4	3
Weight (grams)	278	181	142	90	68	51	35
Wire Diameter (mm)	.97	.84	.79	.69	.63	.58	.53
Bend Resistance (oz.)	76	68	64	52	44	48	40

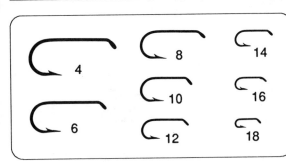

59

Wire: Fine
Shape: Round
Eye: Ball, turned down
Finish: Bronze
Sizes: 4 to 18

Common Uses: Dry flies, nymphs and bass bugs in the larger sizes.

Comment: Style #159 is identical except that it has a turned up eye.

Possible Substitutes: Mustad 94840; Partridge L2A; Kamasan B-400; Tiemco TMC100; VMC 9288

Specifications:

SIZES:	4	6	8	10	12	14	16	18
Shank Length (mm)	18	15	12	10	9	8	6	5
Gape (mm)	9	7.5	7	6	5	4	3	2
Weight (grams)	170	115	75	51	38	26	17	13
Wire Diameter (mm)	.84	.74	.63	.58	.53	.48	.43	.41
Bend Resistance (oz.)	64	30	20	19	17	16	14	15

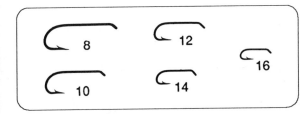

60

Wire: Fine
Shape: Sproat
Eye: Ball, turned down
Finish: Bronze
Sizes: 8 to 16

Common Uses: Dry flies, floating nymphs and emergers.

Possible Substitutes: Partridge E1A

Specifications:

SIZES:	8	10	12	14	16
Shank Length (mm)	14	11	10	8	6
Gape (mm)	6	5	4	3	2.5
Weight (grams)	77	54	36	25	15
Wire Diameter (mm)	.63	.58	.53	.48	.41
Bend Resistance (oz.)	24	25	23	20	12

61

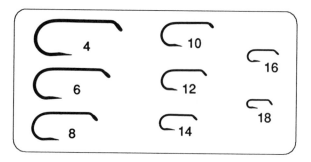

Wire: Fine
Shape: Round
Eye: Ball, turned down
Finish: Bronze
Sizes: 4 to 18

Common Uses: Barbless dry flies, wet flies and nymphs.

Comment: Similar to Eagle Claw #59 except barbless.

Possible Substitutes: Mustad 94845; Partridge E6A

Specifications:

SIZES:	4	6	8	10	12	14	16	18
Shank Length (mm)	17	15	12	10	9	8	6	5
Gape (mm)	9	7.5	7	6	5	4	3	2
Weight (grams)	175	115	72	50	36	24	17	13
Wire Diameter (mm)	.84	.74	.63	.58	.53	.48	.43	.41
Bend Resistance (oz.)	58	34	21	20	17	16	15	15

63

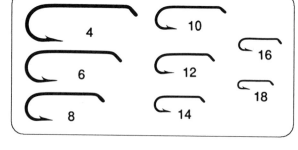

Wire: Regular
Shape: Round
Eye: Ball, turned down
Length: 2X long
Finish: Bronze
Sizes: 4 to 18

Common Uses: Nymphs, muddlers, bucktails, and longer bodied dry flies.

Possible Substitutes: Mustad 9671; Partridge H1A; Kamasan B-830; Tiemco TMC 5262; VMC 9279

Specifications:

SIZES:	4	6	8	10	12	14	16	18
Shank Length (mm)	22	19	15	14	11	10	9	7
Gape (mm)	9	7.5	7	5.5	5	4	3	2
Weight (grams)	255	175	130	85	64	46	25	16
Wire Diameter (mm)	.97	.86	.79	.69	.63	.58	.48	.40
Bend Resistance (oz.)	88	45	42	36	32	28	22	18

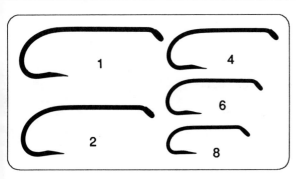

64B

Shape:	Sproat
Eye:	Ball, turned down
Length:	Long
Finish:	Bronze
Sizes:	1 to 8

Common Uses: Barbless salmon and steelhead wet flies and bass flies.
Comment: Same as Eagle Claw #1197 except that this model is barbless. This is the heaviest of the barbless hooks.
Possible Substitutes: None

Specifications:

SIZES:	1	2	4	6	8
Shank Length (mm)	26	24	20	17	15
Gape (mm)	12	11	9.5	8	6
Weight (grams)	650	505	370	250	190
Wire Diameter (mm)	1.32	1.22	1.12	.99	.94
Bend Resistance (oz.)	176	160	148	100	114

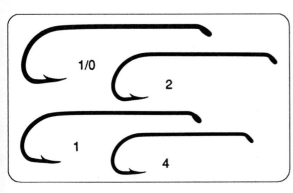

74

Shape:	Forged, Eagle Claw
Eye:	Ball, turned down
Length:	Extra, extra long
Finish:	Gold
Sizes:	4/0 to 4

Common Uses: Saltwater and bass streamers.
Comment: Eagle Claw's model #65CAT is identical except it is cadmium and tin plated. Model #66 series is also similar but with a straight eye, in stainless (#66SS), Nickel (#66N), Cad/Tin (#66CAT), and Bronze (#72).

Specifications:

SIZES:	4/0	3/0	2/0	1/0	1	2	4
Shank Length (mm)	42	41	40	37	35	33	30
Gape (mm)	16	15	14	12	11	10	9
Weight (grams)	1300	1085	880	690	465	390	275
Wire Diameter (mm)	1.55	1.45	1.35	1.24	1.04	.99	.89
Bend Resistance (oz.)	236	208	160	124	82	80	76

159

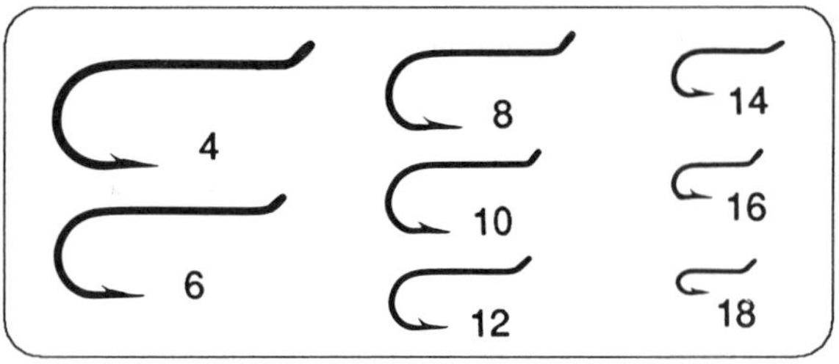

Wire: Extra fine
Shape: Round
Eye: Ball, turned up
Finish: Bronze
Sizes: 4 to 18

Common Uses: Dry flies, nymphs, and wet flies.

Comment: Identical to Eagle Claw #59 except for the turned up eye.

Possible Substitutes: Mustad 94842; VMC 9289

Specifications:

SIZES:	4	6	8	10	12	14	16	18
Shank Length (mm)	16	15	12	10	9	7	6	5
Gape (mm)	8.5	7.5	6.5	6	5	4	3	1.5
Weight (grams)	175	115	73	52	37	26	17	13
Wire Diameter (mm)	.84	.74	.63	.58	.53	.48	.43	.40
Bend Resistance (oz.)	36	26	22	24	22	20	15	20

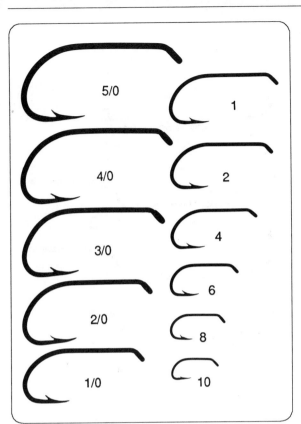

178

Shape:	Forged, Eagle Claw, offset
Eye:	Ball, turned down
Finish:	Gold
Sizes:	5/0 to 10

Common Uses: Bass and saltwater streamers.

Possible Substitutes: Mustad 34007; VMC 9255

Specifications:

SIZES:	5/0	4/0	3/0	2/0	1/0
Shank Length (mm)	26	25	24	22	20
Gape (mm)	17	16	15	14	12
Weight (grams)	1350	1000	885	655	500
Wire Diameter (mm)	1.73	1.52	1.45	1.32	1.22
Bend Resistance (oz.)	248	200	168	148	140

Specifications:

SIZES:	1	2	4	6	8	10
Shank Length (mm)	19	14	13	11	9	7
Gape (mm)	11	10	9	7	6	4.5
Weight (grams)	335	280	195	125	81	58
Wire Diameter (mm)	1.07	.99	.89	.79	.70	.60
Bend Resistance (oz.)	96	80	68	60	48	44

254SS

Shape: Forged, O'Shaughnessy, offset
Eye: Ball, straight
Finish: Stainless steel
Sizes: 5/0 to 6

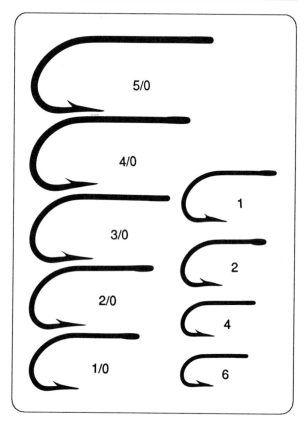

Common Uses: Saltwater and bass streamers.

Possible Substitutes: Mustad 34007; VMC 9255

Specifications:

SIZES:	5/0	4/0	3/0	2/0	1/0
Shank Length (mm)	30	26	20	18	15
Gape (mm)	18	17	16	15	14
Weight (grams)	1640	1325	935	745	570
Wire Diameter (mm)	1.83	1.73	1.52	1.45	1.32
Bend Resistance (oz.)	256	228	172	146	136

Specifications:

SIZES:	1	2	4	6
Shank Length (mm)	12	12	11	10
Gape (mm)	12.5	11	9	8
Weight (grams)	430	385	275	225
Wire Diameter (mm)	1.22	1.22	1.12	1.04
Bend Resistance (oz.)	112	126	130	108

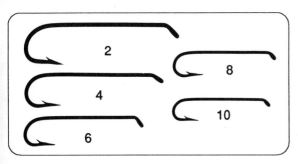

281

Wire:	1X heavy
Shape:	Sproat
Eye:	Ball, turned down
Length:	4X long
Finish:	Bronze
Sizes:	2 to 10

Common Uses: Streamers, bucktails, stonefly nymphs, and in the larger sizes - steelhead flies.

Possible Substitutes: Mustad 33957; Kamasan B-800; Tiemco TMC 300

Specifications:

SIZES:	2	4	6	8	10
Shank Length (mm)	32	29	25	22	21
Gape (mm)	9	7	7	5.5	5
Weight (grams)	465	325	225	155	125
Wire Diameter (mm)	1.12	.99	.89	.78	.74
Bend Resistance (oz.)	128	100	88	64	60

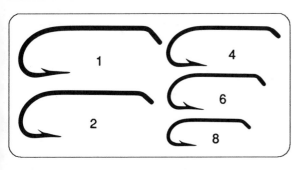

1197B

Shape:	Sproat
Eye:	Ball, turned down
Length:	Long
Finish:	Bronze
Sizes:	1 to 8

Common Uses: Steelhead streamer flies, subsurface bass flies, and saltwater flies on the plated models.
Comment: Also available in nickel plated (1197N), and gold plated (1197G). See also Eagle Claw #64B.
Possible Substitutes: Mustad 7970.

Specifications:

SIZES:	1	2	4	6	8
Shank Length (mm)	26	25	20	17	15
Gape (mm)	12	11	9	8	6
Weight (grams)	660	505	375	255	195
Wire Diameter (mm)	1.32	1.22	1.12	.99	.94
Bend Resistance (oz.)	176	160	120	112	100

B-170

Shape:	Sproat
Eye:	Ball, turned down
Finish:	Bronze
Sizes:	6 to 16

Common Uses: Wet flies, nymphs and heavily hackled dry flies.

Comment: Kamasan offers a similar hook model B-160, but with a 3X short shank. These hooks as well as all Kamasan hooks on the following pages are "chemically sharpened".

Possible Substitutes: Eagle Claw 57; Mustad 3906; Tiemco TMC 100; VMC 8527

Specifications:

SIZES:	6	8	10	12	14	16
Shank Length (mm)	12	11	10	8	6	5
Gape (mm)	7.5	6	5	4	3	2.5
Weight (grams)	98	79	52	44	24	14
Wire Diameter (mm)	.69	.66	.56	.51	.46	.38
Bend Resistance (oz.)	40	44	32	26	24	20

B-180

Shape:	Forged salmon
Eye:	Tapered loop, turned up
Finish:	Black
Sizes:	4 to 12

Common Uses: Low water salmon, regular salmon and steelhead wet flies, stonefly nymphs and matukas.

Possible Substitutes: Mustad 90240; Partridge N; Tiemco TMC 7999

Specifications:

SIZES:	4	6	8	10	12
Shank Length (mm)	23	18	14	12	10
Gape (mm)	8	7.5	6	5.5	5
Weight (grams)	290	190	120	81	55
Wire Diameter (mm)	.97	.86	.76	.66	.61
Bend Resistance (oz.)	1.32	96	88	74	46

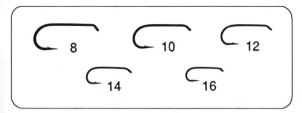

B-400

Shape: Forged round
Eye: Ball, turned down
Finish: Bronzed
Sizes: 8 to 16

K
A
M
A
S
A
N

Common Uses: Traditional and full hackled dry flies, wulffs, humpys, as well as nymphs and light wire wet flies.

Possible Substitutes: Mustad 94840; Tiemco TMC-100; Eagle Claw 59; VMC 9280; Partridge L3A

Specifications:

SIZES:	8	10	12	14	16
Shank Length (mm)	12	10	9	8	7
Gape (mm)	6	5.5	5	4	3
Weight (grams)	80	53	35	24	20
Wire Diameter (mm)	.64	.58	.51	.46	.43
Bend Resistance (oz.)	52	32	28	22	21

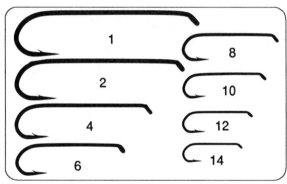

B-800

Shape: Forged, round
Eye: Ball, turned down
Length: 4X long
Finish: Bronze
Sizes: 1 to 14

Common Uses: Streamers, bucktails, stonefly nymphs, muddlers, hoppers
Comment: Kamasan also offers model B-820, in sizes 4 to 12, which is identical except that the eye is straight rather than turned down.
Possible Substitutes: Mustad 79580; Tiemco TMC-300; VMC 9283; Eagle Claw 281; Partridge D4A
Specifications:

SIZE:	1	2	4	6	8	10	12	14
Shank Length (mm)	40	36	28	22	19	17	14	12
Gape (mm)	10	9	8	7	6	5.5	5	4
Weight (grams)	635	500	300	195	135	88	62	41
Wire Diameter (mm)	1.19	1.14	.97	.86	.76	.66	.58	.53
Bend Resistance (oz.)	176	143	116	92	80	58	34	26

B-810

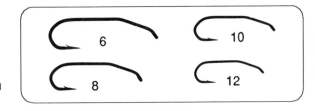

Bend: Forged, round
Eye: Ball, turned down
Length: 4X long
Finish: Bronze
Sizes: 6 to 12

Common Uses: Stonefly and larger mayfly nymphs, also "upside down" lures.

Comment: 20° kink in shank results in special bend. Otherwise appears identical to their model B-800. May be used for "upside down" weedless flies.

Possible Substitutes: None, unless you bend the hook yourself.

Specifications:

SIZE	6	8	10	12
Shank Length (mm)	n/a	n/a	n/a	n/a
Gape (mm)	7	6.5	6	5
Weight (grams)	200	135	88	62
Wire Diameter (mm)	.84	.76	.66	.61
Bend Resistance (oz.)	88	68	48	38

B-830

Bend: Forged, round
Eye: Ball, turned down
Length: 2X long
Finish: Bronze
Sizes: 6 to 14

Common Uses: Bucktails, nymphs, muddlers and grasshoppers

Possible Substitutes: Partridge D4A; Mustad 9672; VMC 9279; Eagle Claw 63; Tiemco 5262

Specifications:

SIZE	6	8	10	12	14
Shank Length (mm)	19	16	14	12	9
Gape (mm)	7	6.5	5.5	5	4.5
Weight (grams)	175	120	80	55	36
Wire Diameter (mm)	.86	.74	.66	.58	.51
Bend Resistance (oz.)	96	72	48	35	26

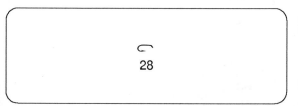

540L

Shape:	Forged, round, offset
Eye:	Ball, turned down
Finish:	Gold
Sizes:	28 only

Common Use: Midges and tiny mayflies.

Possible Substitutes: In bronze only, Mustad 94840 or 94859; Partridge K1A

Specifications:

SIZES:	28
Shank Length (mm)	3
Gape (mm)	1.5
Weight (grams)	.4
Wire Diameter (mm)	.27
Bend Resistance (oz.)	10

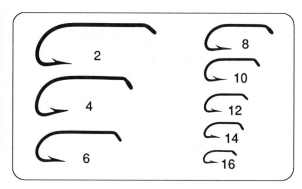

3123

Shape:	Limerick
Eye:	Ball, turned down
Finish:	Bronze
Sizes:	2 to 16

Common Use: Wet flies and nymphs

Possible Substitutes: Mustad 7970 is a similar, but, heavier hook.

Specifications:

SIZES:	2	4	6	8	10	12	14	16
Shank Length (mm)	22	18	14	11	9	6	5	4.5
Gape (mm)	10	8	7	6	5	4	3.5	3
Weight (grams)	315	235	165	105	72	43	35	21
Wire Diameter (mm)	1.01	.91	.84	.73	.66	.56	.51	.43
Bend Resistance (oz.)	112	96	76	60	56	40	35	26

MUSTAD

3257 B

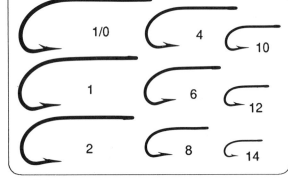

Shape: Sproat
Eye: Tapered, turned down
Finish: Bronze
Sizes: 8 to 16

Common Use: Barbless trout, bass and panfish flies.

Possible Substitutes: No other hooks have this particular barbless configuration.

Specifications:

SIZES:	8	10	12	14	16
Shank Length (mm)	11	9	7	6	5.5
Gape (mm)	6	5	4.5	4	3
Weight (grams)	101	74	47	33	22
Wire Diameter (mm)	.76	.69	.61	.53	.46
Bend Resistance (oz.)	60	41	34	28	19

3366

Shape: Sproat
Eye: Ball, straight
Finish: Bronze
Sizes: 5/0 to 14

Common Use: Wet flies for bass, panfish and trout.
Comment: This is a less expensive hook often used commercialy. Also available in nickel plate (3365A and 3365C) or gold (33602) or blued (3367).

Specifications:

SIZES:	1/0	1	2	4	6	8	10	12	14
Shank Length (mm)	21	20	19	15	11	9	8	7	5
Gape (mm)	13	12	11	9	8	6.5	5.5	4.5	3.5
Weight (grams)	395	305	250	175	125	82	58	36	25
Wire Diameter (mm)	1.07	.99	.94	.81	.76	.67	.60	.53	.46
Bend Resistance (oz.)	112	88	72	68	52	44	40	30	21

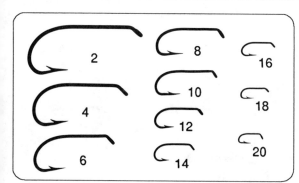

3399 A

Shape:	Sproat
Eye:	Ball, turned down
Finish:	Bronze
Sizes:	2 to 20

Common Use: Wet flies for all gamefish species.
Comment: Model 3399 is similar but with a larger eye and is offered in sizes 9/0 to 20. Also available is Model 3399N (gold plated) in sizes1 to 20.
Possible Substitutes: Eagle Claw 57; VMC 8527

Specifications:

SIZES:	4	6	8	10	12	14	16	18	20
Shank Length (mm)	16	13	12	10	8	6	5	5	4
Gape (mm)	10	7	6	5.5	4.5	4	3	2.5	2.5
Weight (grams)	205	145	100	70	47	28	18	12	9
Wire Diameter (mm)	.89	.81	.74	.63	.58	.48	.41	.36	.33
Bend Resistance (oz.)	68	56	48	34	32	24	19	15	12

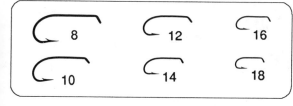

3399 D

Wire:	2 extra fine
Shape:	Sproat
Eye:	Ball, turned down
Finish:	Bronze
Sizes:	8 to 18

Common Use: Dry flies and nymphs.

Possible Substitutes: Eagle Claw 59; VMC 9288

Specifications:

SIZES:	8	10	12	14	16	18
Shank Length (mm)	12	9	8	7	6	5
Gape (mm)	7.5	6	5	4	3.5	2.5
Weight (grams)	71	46	28	17	12	9
Wire Diameter (mm)	.61	.53	.46	.38	.36	.30
Bend Resistance (oz.)	24	21	18	14	9	8

MUSTAD

3582

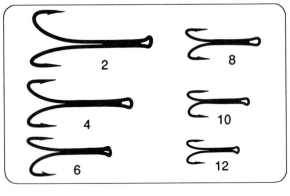

Shape: Salmon
Eye: Looped, turned down
Finish: Bronze
Sizes: 2 to 12

Common Use: Double trout and salmon wet flies.
Possible Substitutes: This is the only double hook being offered with either a down eye or bronze finish.

Specifications:

SIZES:	2	4	6	8	10	12
Shank Length (mm)	20	15	15	12	10	8
Gape (mm)	11	9.5	8	6.5	5	4
Weight (grams)	625	470	320	225	160	105
Wire Diameter (mm)	1.01	.91	.81	.73	.66	.58
Bend Resistance (oz.)	192	152	130	112	88	76

3582 C

Shape: Salmon
Eye: Looped, turned up
Finish: Black
Sizes: 2/0 to 12

Common Use: Atlantic Salmon wet flies.
Comment: For a similar but lighter wire double hook, see Mustad 3582 F.
Possible Substitutes: Partridge P

Specifications:

SIZES:	2/0	1/0	2	4	6	8	10	12
Shank Length (mm)	32	28	25	20	18	13	11	9
Gape (mm)	13	12	9	8	7	6.5	5	4
Weight (grams)	1280	1070	745	435	365	260	170	100
Wire Diameter (mm)	1.22	1.22	1.00	.97	.81	.76	.74	.56
Bend Resistance (oz.)	288	256	208	184	160	132	124	76

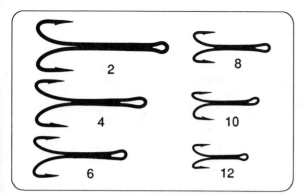

3582F

Shape: Salmon
Eye: Looped, turned up
Finish: Black
Sizes: 2 to 12

Common Use: Atlantic Salmon wet flies.
Comment: For a similar but heavier wire double hook, see Mustad 3582C.
Possible Substitutes: Partridge Q

Specifications:

SIZES:	2	4	6	8	10	12
Shank Length (mm)	26	17	14	12	11	10
Gape (mm)	10	9	8	7	5	4.5
Weight (grams)	665	475	325	225	154	101
Wire Diameter (mm)	1.02	.91	.81	.74	.66	.58
Bend Resistance (oz.)	176	160	128	112	76	64

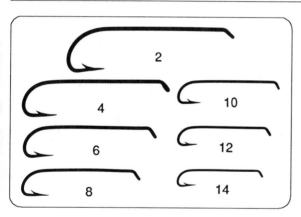

3665A

Shape: Limerick
Eye: Tapered, turned down
Finish: Bronze
Sizes: 2 to 14

Common Use: Streamers, bucktails, large mayfly drys, and nymphs
Possible Substitutes: Mustad 9575; Partridge CS17

Specifications:

SIZES:	2	4	6	8	10	12	14
Shank Length (mm)	33	30	27	24	20	19	18
Gape (mm)	10	8.5	7	6	5	4.5	4
Weight (grams)	385	293	216	154	103	78	54
Wire Diameter (mm)	1.02	.94	.84	.76	.66	.61	.53
Bend Resistance (oz.)	108	88	76	68	54	45	33

3906

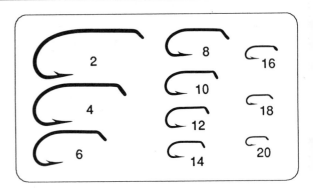

Wire: Standard
Shape: Sproat
Eye: Tapered, turned down
Length: Standard
Finish: Bronze
Sizes: 2 to 20

Common Uses: Wet flies and nymphs.

Comment: In recent years this hook has been the "standard" for traditional wet flies.

Possible Substitutes: Eagle Claw 57; Kamasan B-170; Partridge G3A; VMC 8527

Specifications:

SIZES:	2	4	6	8	10
Shank Length (mm)	18	14	11	10	9
Gape (mm)	11	9	7.5	6	5.5
Weight (grams)	300	225	145	105	69
Wire Diameter (mm)	1.02	.94	.84	.76	.66
Bend Resistance (oz.)	100	80	68	64	52

Specifications:

SIZES:	12	14	16	18	20
Shank Length (mm)	8	6	5	4	3.5
Gape (mm)	4.5	4	3	2	2
Weight (grams)	46	32	18	13	9
Wire Diameter (mm)	.61	.53	.46	.41	.33
Bend Resistance (oz.)	40	37	27	23	18

MUSTAD

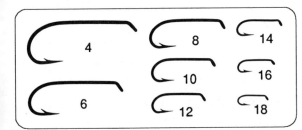

3906 B

Wire: Standard
Shape: Sproat
Eye: Tapered, turned down
Finish: Bronze
Sizes: 4 to 18

Common Use: Mayfly nymphs and wet flies.

Comment: identical to 3906 but 1X long.

Possible Substitutes: Mustad 7957B

Specifications:

SIZES:	4	6	8	10	12	14	16	18
Shank Length (mm)	19	17	14	12	10	8	7	5.5
Gape (mm)	10	8	6.5	5	4	3.5	3	2
Weight (grams)	240	167	109	73	51	35	20	12
Wire Diameter (mm)	.94	.84	.76	.66	.61	.53	.46	.41
Bend Resistance (oz.)	88	64	60	54	42	37	28	20

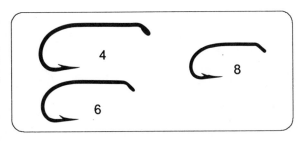

3908

Wire: Extra heavy
Shape: Sproat
Eye: Tapered, turned down
Finish: Bronze
Sizes: 4 to 8

Common Use: Heavy wet flies for salmon, steelhead and bass.

Comment: Also available in nickel plated (3908 C)

Possible Substitutes: Partridge G3A

Specifications:

SIZES:	4	6	8
Shank Length (mm)	13	10	9
Gape (mm)	9	8	6
Weight (grams)	245	170	115
Wire Diameter (mm)	.97	.89	.79
Bend Resistance (oz.)	92	86	80

7948 A

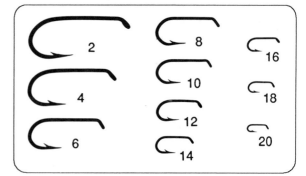

Shape: Forged, round
Eye: Tapered, turned down
Finish: Bronze
Sizes: 2 to 20

Common Use: Dry and wet flies.

Possible Substitutes: Eagle Claw 57; Partridge G3A; VMC 9280

Specifications:

SIZES:	4	6	8	10	12	14	16	18	20
Shank Length (mm)	13	15	12	10	8	7	6	4	4
Gape (mm)	8	7	6	5.5	5	4	3	2.5	1.5
Weight (grams)	210	150	100	64	50	32	19	15	9
Wire Diameter (mm)	.91	.84	.76	.66	.61	.53	.46	.38	.33
Bend Resistance (oz.)	80	72	64	60	46	41	30	23	20

7957 B

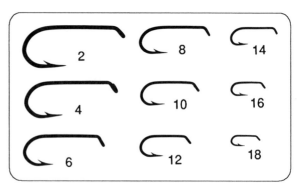

Shape: Forged, round
Eye: Tapered, turned down
Finish: Bronze
Sizes: 2 to 20

Common Use: Full hackled dry flies such as Humpys and Wullfs; also wet flies and nymphs.
Possible Substitutes: Eagle Claw 60; Partridge L2A; VMC 8527

Specifications:

SIZES:	2	4	6	8	10	12	14	16	18
Shank Length (mm)	19	18	16	13	11	9	8	7	6
Gape (mm)	10	8	7	6	5.5	5	4	3	2.5
Weight (grams)	290	210	150	105	74	52	45	20	15
Wire Diameter (mm)	1.02	.94	.84	.76	.66	.61	.53	.46	.41
Bend Resistance (oz.)	92	88	72	68	48	42	30	28	21

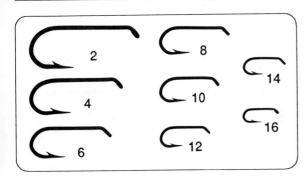

7957 BX

Wire:	Extra strong
Shape:	Forged, round
Eye:	Tapered, turned down
Finish:	Bronze
Sizes:	2 to 16

Common Use: Wet flies and nymphs, also dry flies requiring a very strong hook

Possible Substitutes: Partridge G3A

Specifications:

SIZES:	2	4	6	8	10	12	14	16
Shank Length (mm)	19	16	15	13	9	8	6	6
Gape (mm)	9.5	8	7	6	5.5	4.5	4	3
Weight (grams)	320	240	175	120	80	55	40	26
Wire Diameter (mm)	1.06	.97	.89	.81	.71	.63	.56	.48
Bend Resistance (oz.)	108	100	72	72	59	48	39	28

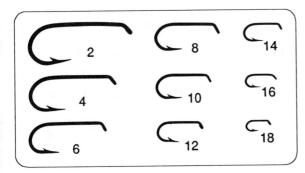

7958

Shape:	Forged, round, offset
Eye:	Tapered, turned down
Finish:	Bronze
Sizes:	2/0 to 18

Common Use: Wet flies and nymphs.

Possible Substitutes: Partridge A; VMC 9282

Specifications:

SIZES:	2	4	6	8	10	12	14	16	18
Shank Length (mm)	18	17	15	12	10	8	6	4.5	4
Gape (mm)	9.5	7.5	7	6	5	4.5	4	3	2
Weight (grams)	295	200	140	105	67	52	33	19	14
Wire Diameter (mm)	.99	.94	.84	.73	.66	.58	.51	.43	.38
Bend Resistance (oz.)	88	80	68	56	36	32	30	22	20

MUSTAD

7970

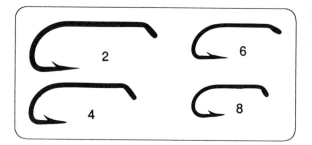

Wire: 5 extra strong
Shape: Limerick
Eye: Ball, turned down
Finish: Bronze
Sizes: 2 to 8

Common Use: Steelhead and bass wet flies.

Comment: This hook is often preferred for its extra weight.

Possible Substitutes: Eagle Claw 1197B

Specifications:

SIZES:	2	4	6	8
Shank Length (mm)	23	18	17	14
Gape (mm)	11	9	8	7
Weight (grams)	685	455	275	225
Wire Diameter (mm)	1.42	1.24	1.07	.99
Bend Resistance (oz.)	216	184	116	104

9049

Wire: Fine
Shape: Dublin, forged
Eye: Looped, oval
turned up
Length: Extra long
Finish: Black
Sizes: 2 to 10

Common Use: Atlantic Salmon and steelhead dry flies and low water style wet flies.

Possible Substitutes: Tiemco 7999; Partridge 01

Specifications:

SIZES:	2	4	6	8	10
Shank Length (mm)	24	20	16.5	15	12
Gape (mm)	10	8.5	7.5	7	5
Weight (grams)	350	280	195	135	86
Wire Diameter (mm)	1.01	.91	.85	.76	.66
Bend Resistance (oz.)	116	100	88	64	56

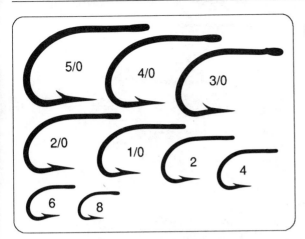

9174

Wire: Extra strong
Shape: Forged, O'Shaughnessy
Eye: Ball, straight
Length: 3X short
Finish: Bronze
Sizes: 5/0 to 8

Common Use: Saltwater streamers ; also "glow bug" egg flies in smaller sizes.
Comment: Model 9175 is identical but cadmium plated and tinned.
Specifications:

SIZES:	5/0	4/0	3/0	2/0	1/0	2	4	6	8
Shank Length (mm)	n/a	n/a	n/a	n/a	n/a	n/a	n/a	n/a	n/a
Gape (mm)	18	16	15	13	11.5	9.5	8	7	6
Weight (grams)	1,340	950	810	620	480	320	205	145	89
Wire Diameter (mm)	1.80	1.60	1.55	1.40	1.32	1.14	1.02	.91	.79
Bend Resistance (oz.)	304	256	244	240	208	164	128	108	72

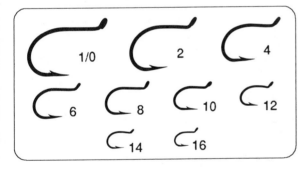

9523

Wire: Extra Fine
Shape: Forged, round, offset
Eye: Tapered, turned up
Length: 5X short
Finish: Bronze
Sizes: 3/0 to 16

Common Use: Spider dry flies using the smaller sizes; also shrimp patterns.
Comment: Mustad offers a similar gold plated hook (9522S - salmon egg) with one slice in the shank which can be removed for fly tying purposes.
Possible Substitutes: Mustad 94843 is only slightly longer.

Specifications:

SIZES:	1/0	2	4	6	8	10	12	14	16
Shank Length (mm)	n/a	n/a	n/a	n/a	n/a	n/a	n/a	n/a	n/a
Gape (mm)	11	10	8.5	7	6.5	5.5	5	4	3
Weight (grams)	255	185	135	91	75	46	29	17	12
Wire Diameter (mm)	1.00	.90	.81	.74	.66	.58	.53	.46	.41
Bend Resistance (oz.)	80	68	60	48	38	27	24	20	16

9575

Shape: Forged, Limerick
Eye: Tapered, looped, turned down
Length: 1/2" longer than regular
Finish: Bronze
Sizes: 2 to 12

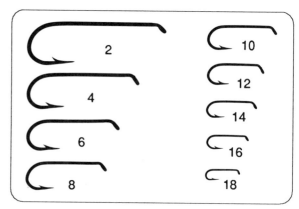

Common Use: Streamers and bucktails
Comment: This is the classic style hook for long shank eastern streamers. The looped eye is often preferred as it avoids the possibility of having the leader suffer abrasion against the wire's cut end at the hook's eye.
Possible Substitutes: Partridge CS17
Specifications:

SIZES:	2	4	6	8	10	12
Shank Length (mm)	34	30	26	25	23	20
Gape (mm)	10	8	7	6.5	5	4.5
Weight (grams)	395	320	230	165	110	81
Wire Diameter (mm)	1.07	.97	.86	.76	.66	.61
Bend Resistance (oz.)	112	88	76	64	56	53

9671

Shape: Forged, round
Eye: Tapered, turned down
Length: 2X long
Finish: Bronze
Sizes: 2 to 18

Common Use: Dry flies, nymphs and grasshoppers.
Possible Substitutes: Eagle Claw 63; Partridge D4A; Tiemco TMC 5262; VMC 9279
Specifications:

SIZES:	2	4	6	8	10	12	14	16	18
Shank Length (mm)	27	23	18	16	14	11	10	9	7
Gape (mm)	9.5	8	7	6	5.5	5	4	3	2.5
Weight (grams)	340	240	170	125	85	65	37	23	14
Wire Diameter (mm)	1.02	.94	.84	.76	.66	.61	.53	.46	.41
Bend Resistance (oz.)	88	84	72	64	48	36	28	23	20

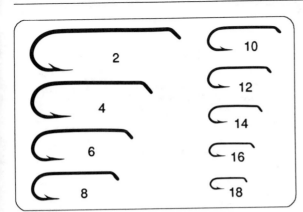

9672

Shape:	Forged, round
Eye:	Tapered, turned down
Length:	3X long
Finish:	Bronze
Sizes:	2 to 18

Common Uses: Bucktails and muddlers.
Possible Substitutes: Eagle Claw 58; Kamasan B-830; Partridge D4A; Tiemco 5263; VMC 9283

Specifications:

SIZES:	2	4	6	8	10	12	14	16	18
Shank Length (mm)	32	25	20	18	14	12	11	9	7
Gape (mm)	9.5	8.5	7	6	5.5	5	4	3	2.5
Weight (grams)	370	260	185	130	85	62	38	24	15
Wire Diameter (mm)	1.02	.94	.84	.76	.66	.61	.53	.46	.41
Bend Resistance (oz.)	96	84	68	64	46	38	32	28	22

MUSTAD

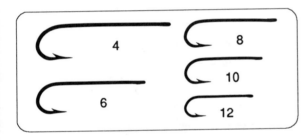

9674

Shape:	Forged, round
Eye:	Ball, straight
Length:	4X long
Finish:	Bronze
Sizes:	4 to 12

Common Uses: Streamers, bucktails and stonefly nymphs.

Possible Substitutes: Partridge D4A; VMC 9148

Specifications:

SIZES:	4	6	8	10	12
Shank Length (mm)	27	23	18	15	14
Gape (mm)	8	7	6	6	5
Weight (grams)	270	190	130	92	64
Wire Diameter (mm)	.94	.84	.76	.66	.61
Bend Resistance (oz.)	84	76	60	44	40

33903

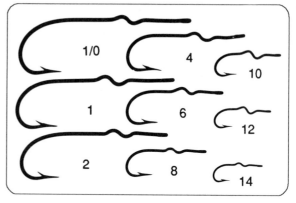

Shape: Sproat
Eye: Ball, straight
Length: Extra long
Finish: Bronze
Sizes: 1/0 to 14

Common Uses: Cork, balsa wood, and plastic bodied poppers for bass and panfish.

Comment: The kinked hook shank prevents the popper body from twisting.

Possible Substitutes: Mustad 33900 is similar but with a single bump.

Specifications:

SIZES:	1/0	1	2	4	6	8	10	12	14
Shank Length (mm)	33	31	27	24	18	15	12	10	9
Gape (mm)	13	11.5	11	8.5	8	6	5	4.5	4
Weight (grams)	430	370	310	210	145	97	66	45	40
Wire Diameter (mm)	1.02	.99	.94	.89	.76	.66	.61	.53	.50
Bend Resistance (oz.)	80	76	72	60	42	37	32	29	26

33957

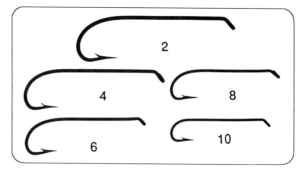

Shape: Sproat
Eye: Ball, turned down
Length: 1/2" longer than regular
Finish: Bronze
Sizes: 2 to 10

Common Uses: Streamers, bucktails, grasshoppers and muddlers.

Possible Substitutes: Eagle Claw 281

Specifications:

SIZES:	2	4	6	8	10
Shank Length (mm)	31	28	24	22	21
Gape (mm)	10	9	8	7	5
Weight (grams)	390	290	200	150	100
Wire Diameter (mm)	1.02	.94	.84	.76	.66
Bend Resistance (oz.)	104	96	68	60	52

M
U
S
T
A
D

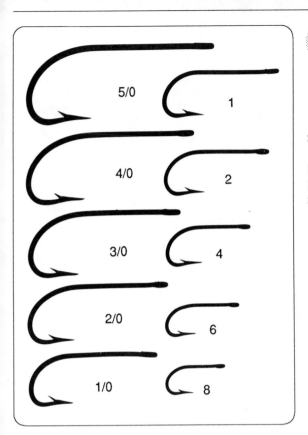

34007

Shape: Forged, O'Shaughnessy
Eye: Ball, straight
Finish: Stainless steel
Sizes: 5/0 to 8

Common Uses: Saltwater streamers and bucktails.

Comment: Because of it's rust and corrosion resistance, this has become the most commonly used hook for saltwater flies.

Possible Substitutes: Eagle Claw 254SS; VMC 9255

Specifications:

SIZES:	5/0	4/0	3/0	2/0	1/0
Shank Length (mm)	33	30	27	24	21
Gape (mm)	18	16	15	13	12
Weight (grams)	1300	860	720	640	515
Wire Diameter (mm)	1.60	1.40	1.40	1.30	1.24
Bend Resistance (oz.)	248	168	160	184	168

Specifications:

SIZES:	1	2	4	6	8
Shank Length (mm)	20	18	14	11	8
Gape (mm)	11	10	9	7	6
Weight (grams)	395	310	220	155	110
Wire Diameter (mm)	1.12	1.00	.97	.89	.75
Bend Resistance (oz.)	136	112	100	92	84

36620

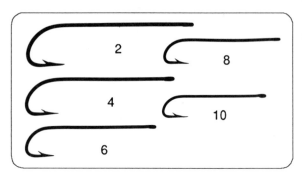

Shape: Limerick
Eye: Ball, straight
Length: 1/2" longer than regular
Finish: Bronze
Sizes: 2 to 10

Common Uses: "Thundercreek" style streamers.

Possible Substitutes: Partridge CS 5

Specifications:

SIZES:	2	4	6	8	10
Shank Length (mm)	33	31	28	25	22
Gape (mm)	10	9	7	6	5
Weight (grams)	400	295	215	150	110
Wire Diameter (mm)	1.01	.94	.84	.76	.66
Bend Resistance (oz.)	104	88	84	60	44

MUSTAD

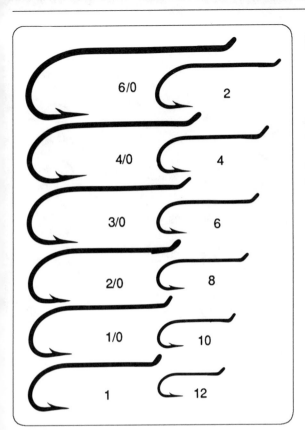

36890

Shape: Forged, Limerick
Eye: Looped, oval, turned up
Finish: Black
Sizes: 6/0 to 12

Common Uses: Atlantic Salmon and Steelhead wet flies.

Possible Substitutes: Partridge M; Tiemco 7999

Specifications:

SIZES:	6/0	4/0	3/0	2/0	1/0
Shank Length (mm)	40	34	31	28	27
Gape (mm)	16	14	13.5	12.5	11.5
Weight (grams)	1400	950	695	585	520
Wire Diameter (mm)	1.65	1.50	1.35	1.27	1.19
Bend Resistance (oz.)	248	192	176	168	160

Specifications:

SIZES:	1	2	4	6	8	10	12
Shank Length (mm)	26	24	23	21	17	15	13
Gape (mm)	11	10	8.5	7.5	7	6	5.5
Weight (grams)	455	390	320	245	170	125	89
Wire Diameter (mm)	1.17	1.14	1.02	.94	.85	.76	.66
Bend Resistance (oz.)	156	148	116	112	80	64	52

37160

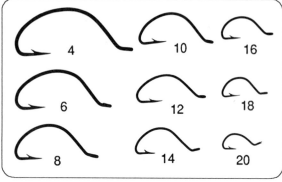

Shape: Wide gap, offset
Eye: Ball, turned up
Finish: Bronze
Sizes: 3/0 to 20

Common Uses: Caddis larva and pupa; shrimp patterns, other nymphs.
Comment: Also available in gold (37162) and nickel (37161).
Possible Substitutes: Mustad offers a similar hook, Model 37140, with a straight ball eye. Also Partridge K2B.

Specifications:

SIZES:	4	6	8	10	12	14	16	18	20
Shank Length (mm)	n/a	n/a	n/a	n/a	n/a	n/a	n/a	n/a	n/a
Gape (mm)	10	9	8	7	6.5	6	5	4.5	4
Weight (grams)	315	210	150	110	80	67	52	49	28
Wire Diameter (mm)	.99	.89	.79	.71	.64	.61	.56	.53	.48
Bend Resistance (oz.)	100	80	64	48	36	32	27	36	25

37187

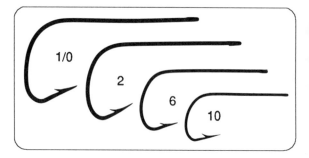

Shape: Open bend
Eye: Ball, straight
Finish: Bronze
Sizes: 1/0,2,6,10

Common Uses: Deer hair and other bass bugs.
Comment: This is known as the "Stinger" hook.
Possible Substitutes: No other hook manufacturer offers this particular hook configuration.

Specifications:

SIZES:	1/0	2	6	10
Shank Length (mm)	33	31	26	20
Gape (mm)	17	15	13	11
Weight (grams)	590	440	245	130
Wire Diameter (mm)	1.12	1.02	.84	.66
Bend Resistance (oz.)	96	88	68	32

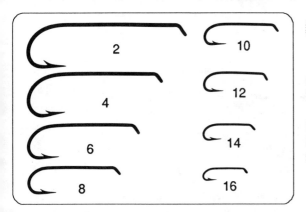

38941

Shape: Sproat
Eye: Tapered, turned down
Length: 3X long
Finish: Bronze
Sizes: 2 to 16

Common Uses: Bucktails, muddlers and stonefly nymphs.
Comment: The sproat bend can add a graceful line to flies which require a 3X long shank.
Possible Substitutes: Eagle Claw 58; Partridge D4A; Mustad 9672
Specifications:

SIZES:	2	4	6	8	10	12	14	16
Shank Length (mm)	33	26	21	19	14	12	9	8
Gape (mm)	10.5	10	9	6.5	5	4.5	4	3
Weight (grams)	375	290	190	125	83	57	38	24
Wire Diameter (mm)	1.02	.94	.84	.76	.66	.61	.53	.46
Bend Resistance (oz.)	100	84	68	56	50	41	30	28

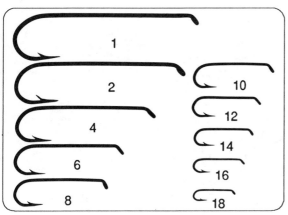

79580

Shape: Forged, round
Eye: Tapered, turned down
Length: 4X long
Finish: Bronze
Sizes: 1 to 18

Common Uses: Streamers, bucktails and stonefly nymphs.
Possible Substitutes: Eagle Claw 281; Kamasan B-800; Tiemco TMC 300; VMC 9283
Specifications:

SIZES:	2	4	6	8	10	12	14	16	18
Shank Length (mm)	37	28	23	20	16	14	12	10	8
Gape (mm)	9	8	7	6	5.5	4.5	3	3	2.5
Weight (grams)	405	285	180	145	90	62	44	37	17
Wire Diameter (mm)	1.02	.94	.84	.76	.66	.61	.53	.45	.40
Bend Resistance (oz.)	88	84	76	60	52	40	36	29	24

MUSTAD

79582

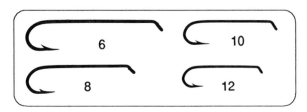

Shape: Forged, round
Eye: Tapered, turned down
Length: 5X long
Finish: Bronze
Sizes: 6 to 12

Common Uses: Streamers, bucktails and large stonefly nymphs.

Comment: Same as 79580 but 5X long.

Possible Substitutes: Tiemco TMC 300

Specifications:

SIZES:	6	8	10	12
Shank Length (mm)	28	23	19	16
Gape (mm)	7	6	5.5	5
Weight (grams)	220	145	105	71
Wire Diameter (mm)	.86	.76	.71	.61
Bend Resistance (oz.)	72	60	48	44

79666

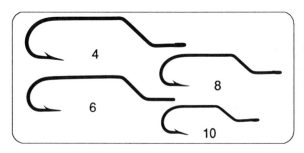

Shape: Forged, round
Eye: Ball, straight
Finish: Bronze
Sizes: 4 to 10

Common Uses: Weedless "keel style" or "upside-down" flies.
Comment: This is known as the "Keel" hook, and is also available in sizes 14 and 16 as model # 38972.
Possible Substitutes: No other hook manufacturer offers this particular hook configuration.

Specifications:

SIZES:	4	6	8	10
Shank Length (mm)	n/a	n/a	n/a	n/a
Gape (mm)	10	8.5	8	7
Weight (grams)	335	250	170	100
Wire Diameter (mm)	.94	.86	.76	.66
Bend Resistance (oz.)	80	72	56	44

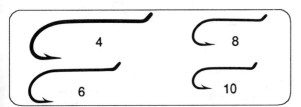

90240

Wire:	2X fine
Shape:	Limerick
Eye:	Looped, turned up
Length:	Extra long
Finish:	Black
Sizes:	4 to 10

Common Uses: Low water style salmon and steelhead wet flies; also dry flies.

Possible Substitutes: Kamasan B- 180; Partridge N

Specifications:

SIZES:	4	6	8	10
Shank Length (mm)	23	17	13	12
Gape (mm)	9	8	6.5	5
Weight (grams)	275	130	86	67
Wire Diameter (mm)	.94	.74	.64	.61
Bend Resistance (oz.)	100	52	48	44

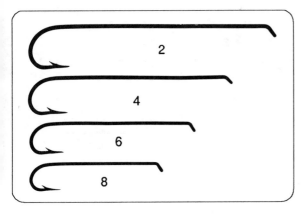

94720

Shape:	Forged, round
Eye:	Tapered, turned down
Finish:	Bronze
Length:	8X long
Sizes:	2 to 8

Common Uses: Trolling streamers; also very large stonefly nymphs.
Possible Substitutes: Partridge CS15

Specifications:

SIZES:	2	4	6	8
Shank Length (mm)	58	46	37	27
Gape (mm)	10	9	7	6.5
Weight (grams)	535	370	250	170
Wire Diameter (mm)	1.07	.94	.84	.76
Bend Resistance (oz.)	96	76	68	60

MUSTAD

94831

Wire: 2X fine
Shape: Forged, round
Eye: Tapered, turned down
Length: 2X long
Finish: Bronze
Sizes: 4 to 16

Common Uses: Large mayfly dry flies; grasshoppers.

Possible Substitutes: Partridge H1A; VMC 9279

Specifications:

SIZES:	4	6	8	10	12	14	16
Shank Length (mm)	22	19	18	14	13	11	9
Gape (mm)	9	7	6	5.5	5	4	3
Weight (grams)	180	120	85	58	37	25	17
Wire Diameter (mm)	.81	.71	.63	.56	.48	.43	.38
Bend Resistance (oz.)	64	56	38	31	21	17	16

94833

Wire: 3X fine
Shape: Forged, round
Eye: Tapered, turned down
Finish: Bronze
Sizes: 6 to 22

Common Uses: No hackle and sparsely dressed dry flies; also floating nymphs, standard dry flies, and ant patterns.

Possible Substitutes: Partridge L4A; Tiemco TMC 5210; VMC 9288

Specifications:

SIZES:	6	8	10	12	14	16	18	20	22
Shank Length (mm)	15	12	10	9	8	7	5	5	4
Gape (mm)	7	6.5	6	5	4	3	2.5	2	1.5
Weight (grams)	91	69	45	28	20	13	8	6	4
Wire Diameter (mm)	.66	.63	.53	.46	.41	.36	.34	.34	.28
Bend Resistance (oz.)	39	34	29	22	15	12	17	15	12

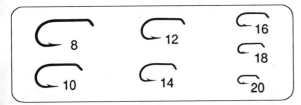

94836

Wire: Extra fine
Shape: Forged, round
Eye: Tapered, turned down
Length: Short shank
Finish: Bronze
Sizes: 10 to 20

Common Uses: Traditional dry flies and variants.

Possible Substitutes: Partridge L3A; VMC 9288

Specifications:

SIZES:	10	12	14	16	18	20
Shank Length (mm)	9	8	7	5	5	4
Gape (mm)	5.5	5	4	3	2	2
Weight (grams)	57	37	25	16	11	7
Wire Diameter (mm)	.58	.53	.43	.38	.33	.32
Bend Resistance (oz.)	32	27	23	16	14	13

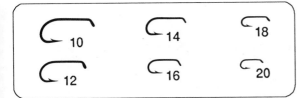

94838

Wire: Extra fine
Shape: Forged, round
Eye: Tapered, turned down
Length: Extra short
Finish: Bronze
Sizes: 8 to 20

Common Uses: Dry flies, extended body dry flies, and beetles.

Possible Substitutes: Partridge E6A; Mustad 94836; VMC 9288

Specifications:

SIZES:	8	10	12	14	16	18	20
Shank Length (mm)	10	8	8	6	5	5	4
Gape (mm)	6	5.5	5	4	3	2	2
Weight (grams)	77	52	36	22	15	10	7
Wire Diameter (mm)	.66	.58	.53	.46	.41	.36	.32
Bend Resistance (oz.)	40	30	26	20	19	17	11

94840

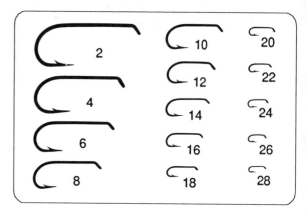

Wire: Standard
Shape: Forged, round
Eye: Tapered, turned down
Length: Standard
Finish: Bronze
Sizes: 2 to 28

Common Uses: Dry flies and nymphs; larger sizes are used for floating bass bugs.

Comment: This hook is considered the "standard" dry fly hook against which all other dry fly hooks are often compared.

Possible Substitutes: Eagle Claw 59; Kamasan B-400; Partridge L2A; Tiemco TMC 5210; VMC 9288

Specifications:

SIZES:	2	4	6	8	10	12	14
Shank Length (mm)	20	17	16	12	11	8	7
Gape (mm)	10	9	7	6	5.5	5	4
Weight (grams)	240	175	120	80	56	41	25
Wire Diameter (mm)	.97	.84	.76	.66	.63	.53	.46
Bend Resistance (oz.)	76	60	52	48	32	26	23

Specifications:

SIZES:	16	18	20	22	24	26	28
Shank Length (mm)	7	6	5	4.5	4	3.5	3
Gape (mm)	3	2.5	2	2	2	2	1.5
Weight (grams)	16	12	8	7	5.5	5	3.5
Wire Diameter (mm)	.41	.36	.32	.30	.29	.28	.27
Bend Resistance (oz.)	16	19	14	12	10	9	9

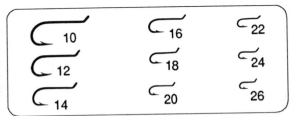

94842

Wire:	Regular
Shape:	Forged, round
Eye:	Tapered, turned up
Finish:	Bronze
Sizes:	8 to 28

Common Uses: Dry flies.
Comment: Identical to # 94840 except the eye is turned up. Some fly tyers prefer the upturned eye on smaller hooks as it helps to keep the smaller gape unobstructed for better hook penetration.
Possible Substitutes: Eagle Claw 159; VMC 9281

Specifications:

SIZES:	10	12	14	16	18	20	22	24	26
Shank Length (mm)	11	9	8	7	6	5	4	4	3.5
Gape (mm)	5.5	5	4	3	2.5	2	2	2	1.5
Weight (grams)	56	40	25	17	12	8	7	5	4
Wire Diameter (mm)	.63	.53	.46	.41	.36	.32	.30	.29	.28
Bend Resistance (oz.)	34	26	25	17	16	14	13	13	12

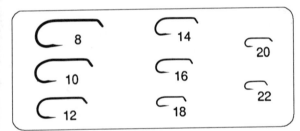

94845

Wire:	Regular
Shape:	Forged, round
Eye:	Tapered, turned down
Finish:	Bronze
Sizes:	8 to 22

Common Uses: Barbless dry flies and nymphs.

Comment: Identical to # 94840 except barbless.

Possible Substitutes: Eagle Claw 61; Partridge E1AY

Specifications:

SIZES:	8	10	12	14	16	18	20	22
Shank Length (mm)	12	11	10	8	7	6	5	4
Gape (mm)	6	5.5	5	4	3	2.5	2	2
Weight (grams)	85	57	40	25	17	11	8	7
Wire Diameter (mm)	.66	.63	.53	.46	.41	.36	.32	.30
Bend Resistance (oz.)	44	34	24	20	18	15	13	12

MUSTAD

94859

Wire:	Extra fine
Shape:	Forged, round
Eye:	Ball, straight
Finish:	Bronze
Sizes:	20 to 28

Common Uses: Small dry flies and midge pupae.

Comment: The straight eye is designed to maximize point clearance in these small sizes, resulting in improved hooking qualities.

Possible Substitutes: Partridge K1A

Specifications:

SIZES:	20	22	24	26	28
Shank Length (mm)	5	4	4	3.5	3
Gape (mm)	2.5	2	2	1.5	1.5
Weight (grams)	8	7	5	4	3
Wire Diameter (mm)	.30	.30	.28	.28	.27
Bend Resistance (oz.)	11	12	11	8	10

94863

Wire:	Standard
Shape:	Forged, round
Eye:	Looped, oval, turned up
Finish:	Bronze
Sizes:	8 to 14

Common Uses: Barbless wet flies, nymphs, and dry flies.

Possible Substitutes: No other hook meets this design standard.

Specifications:

SIZES:	8	10	12	14
Shank Length (mm)	12	10	9	8
Gape (mm)	6	5.5	5	4
Weight (grams)	80	66	45	23
Wire Diameter (mm)	.63	.61	.53	.46
Bend Resistance (oz.)	36	32	22	18

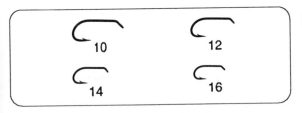

A

Wire: 2X fine
Shape: Offset, improved sproat
Eye: Ball, turned down
Length: 1X short
Finish: Bronze
Sizes: 10 to 16

Common Uses: Standard and soft hackle wet flies; short bodied nymphs.

Comment: The offset bend, while not commonly found in fly tying hooks, is designed to aid in hook penetration.

Possible Substitutes: Mustad 7958; VMC 9282

Specifications:

SIZES:	10	12	14	16
Shank Length (mm)	8.5	7	5.5	5
Gape (mm)	5.5	4.5	4	3.5
Weight (grams)	54	36	26	18
Wire Diameter (mm)	.61	.56	.51	.46
Bend Resistance (oz.)	46	40	31	26

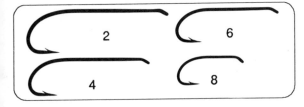

CS2 SH

Wire: Heavy
Shape: Forged salmon
Eye: Tapered loop, turned down
Finish: Black
Sizes: 2,4,6,8

Common Uses: Steelhead wet flies, streamers and bucktails.

Comment: This hook is described as the SEB Steelhead Hook, and is available in black finish (BL) or silver finish (SL). The looped eye is designed to eliminate any roughness at the eye, and thus reduce the probability of leader breakage.

Possible Substitutes: No other hooks offer all of the same characteristics.

Specifications:

SIZES:	2	4	6	8
Shank Length (mm)	27	23	20	15
Gape (mm)	10.0	8.5	8.0	7.0
Weight (grams)	340	255	180	120
Wire Diameter (mm)	1.02	.90	.83	.74
Bend Resistance (oz.)	136	128	88	80

CS5

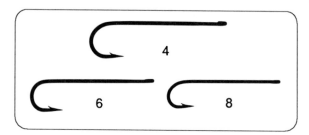

Wire: Heavy
Shape: Round
Eye: Ball, straight
Length: 2X long
Finish: Blued
Sizes: 4,6 8

Common Uses: This is the type of straight eye hook specified for tying the "Thundercreek" series of bucktails and streamers.
Comment: This hook is also known as the "Fulsher Thundercreek", named for Keith Fulsher who wrote the book *Fishing the Thundercreek Series*.

Possible Substitutes: Mustad 36620

Specifications:

SIZES:	4	6	8
Shank Length (mm)	30	28	25
Gape (mm)	8.5	7.5	6.5
Weight (grams)	320	250	200
Wire Diameter (mm)	1.00	.93	.89
Bend Resistance (oz.)	100	96	84

CS6

Wire: Heavy
Shape: Dublin salmon
Eye: None
Finish: Black
Sizes: 4/0 only

Common Uses: Traditional Atlantic Salmon flies tied for display, rather than actual fishing purposes.
Comment: Described by Partridge as the "Adlington & Hutchinson Blind Eye Salmon Hook", an eye is added by forming a loop of twisted strands of gut, and securing it to the hook. The point of this hook is hand filed.
Possible Substitutes: None

Specifications:

SIZE:	4/0
Shank Length (mm)	n/a
Gape (mm)	16
Weight (grams)	730
Wire Diameter (mm)	1.40
Bend Resistance (oz.)	232

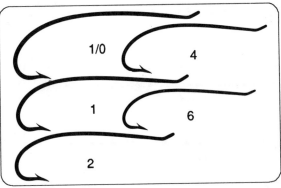

CS10

Wire:	Medium
Shape:	Forged "Dublin Bartleet" Salmon
Eye:	Tapered loop, turned up
Length:	2X long
Finish:	Black
Sizes:	1/0, 1, 2, 4, 6

Common Uses: Traditional or classic Atlantic Salmon flies, for both actual use as well as for display purposes. Also Steelhead and Sea Trout flies.

Comment: Many fly tyers prefer the traditional graceful curve of this hook over the more readily available salmon hooks.

Possible Substitutes: None except for the Partridge CS6 Blind eye hook

Specifications:

SIZES:	1/0	1	2	4	6
Shank Length (mm)	n/a	n/a	n/a	n/a	n/a
Gape (mm)	14	12	11	10	9
Weight (grams)	525	435	365	280	195
Wire Diameter (mm)	1.09	1.05	1.02	.91	.80
Bend Resistance (oz.)	144	136	128	124	76

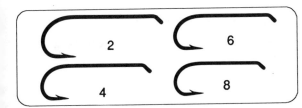

CS11

Wire:	Standard
Shape:	Forged "Redditch"
Eye:	Ball, turned down
Length:	4X long
Finish:	Stainless steel
Sizes:	2, 4, 6, 8

Common Uses: Saltwater or brackish water streamers; or other long bodied flies which require a silver color hook.

Comment: This is a stainless steel version of the Partridge D4A Bucktail and Streamer hook.

Possible Substitutes: VMC 9148

Specifications:

SIZES:	2	4	6	8
Shank Length (mm)	24	22	20	18
Gape (mm)	10	8.5	8	7.5
Weight (grams)	270	205	195	170
Wire Diameter (mm)	.91	.86	.86	.81
Bend Resistance (oz.)	88	72	68	60

PARTRIDGE

CS15

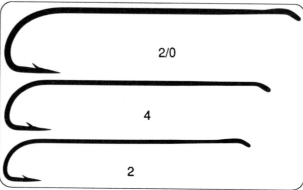

Wire: Heavy
Shape: Limerick
Eye: Tapered loop, turned down
Length: Extra long
Finish: Bronze
Sizes: 2/0, 2, 4

Common Uses: Trolling streamers such as those commonly used in New England and Eastern Canada. Also Alaskan and Great Lakes streamers.
Comment: Known as the "Carrie Stevens Trolling Hook" since it was a hook similar to this on which she originated many flies, including the Grey Ghost.
Possible Substitutes: Mustad 94720
Specifications:

SIZES:	2/0	2	4
Shank Length (mm)	65	60	55
Gape (mm)	14	11.5	10
Weight (grams)	1470	930	600
Wire Diameter (mm)	1.57	1.32	1.10
Bend Resistance (oz.)	288	192	144

CS17

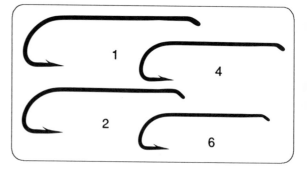

Wire: Heavy
Shape: Limerick
Eye: Tapered loop, turned down
Length: 6X long
Finish: Black
Sizes: 1, 2, 4, 6

Common Uses: Streamers, bucktails
Comment: Also known as the "Bob John's" hook. Size #8 to be soon offered.
Possible Substitutes: Mustad 9575

Specifications:

SIZES:	1	2	4	6
Shank Length (mm)	38	33	30	27
Gape (mm)	12	11	9	8.5
Weight (grams)	540	450	350	260
Wire Diameter (mm)	1.16	1.10	1.02	.92
Bend Resistance (oz.)	148	140	128	112

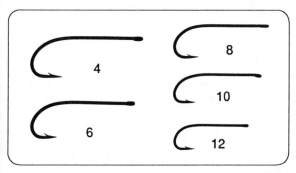

D3ST

Wire: Heavyweight
Shape: Forged salmon
Eye: Straight ball
Length: 4X long
Finish: Bronze
Sizes: 4 to 12

Common Uses: Streamers, bucktails, muddlers, and any fly which requires a long shank hook with a straight eye.
Comment: Partridge describes this as "a strong hook designed for big fish".
Possible Substitutes: Kamasan B-800

Specifications:

SIZES:	4	6	8	10	12
Shank Length (mm)	20	18	17	14	12
Gape (mm)	9	8	8	6.5	6
Weight (grams)	200	185	130	90	70
Wire Diameter (mm)	.83	.83	.76	.66	.61
Bend Resistance (oz.)	72	88	44	39	36

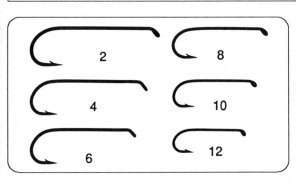

D4A

Wire: Heavyweight
Shape: Forged Redditch
Eye: Ball, turned down
Length: 4X long
Finish: Bronze
Sizes: 2 to 12

Common Uses: Bucktails, streamers, stonefly nymphs, muddlers and grasshoppers
Possible Substitutes: Eagle Claw 58; Kamasan B-800; Mustad 9671; VMC 9279

Specifications:

SIZES:	2	4	6	8	10	12
Shank Length (mm)	25	23	20	18	17	14
Gape (mm)	9.5	9	8.5	8	7	6
Weight (grams)	250	185	170	130	95	70
Wire Diameter (mm)	.89	.81	.81	.74	.66	.61
Bend Resistance (oz.)	88	64	68	48	39	32

E1A

Wire:	4X fine
Shape:	Forged Redditch
Eye:	Ball, turned down
Length:	1/2X long
Finish:	Bronze
Sizes:	10 to 18

Common Uses: Traditional dry flies and floating nymphs.

Comment: Called the "Hooper Long Shank Dry" and once sold as the Orvis "Premium" hook. Also manufactured in a barbless form under code E3AY.

Possible Substitutes: Eagle Claw 60; Mustad 94840; VMC 9280

Specifications:

SIZES:	10	12	14	16	18
Shank Length (mm)	12	10	8	7.5	6
Gape (mm)	6	5	4	3.5	3
Weight (grams)	50	41	25	20	14
Wire Diameter (mm)	.56	.51	.46	.41	.36
Bend Resistance (oz.)	27	29	23	22	19

E3AY

Wire:	4X fine
Shape:	Forged Redditch
Eye:	Ball, turned down
Length:	1/2X long
Finish:	Bronze
Sizes:	10 to 18

Common Uses: Barbless traditional dry flies and floating nymphs.

Comment: This hook is identical to Code E1A except that this is barbless.

Possible Substitutes: Eagle Claw 61; Mustad 94845

Specifications:

SIZES:	10	12	14	16	18
Shank Length (mm)	12	10	8	7.5	6
Gape (mm)	6	5	4	3.5	3
Weight (grams)	50	41	25	20	14
Wire Diameter (mm)	.56	.51	.46	.41	.36
Bend Resistance (oz.)	27	29	23	22	19

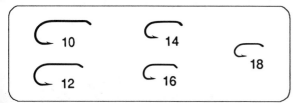

Wire: 4X fine
Shape: Forged Redditch
Eye: Ball, turned down
Length: 1X short
Finish: Bronze
Sizes: 10 to 18

Common Uses: Dry flies, variants, extended body mayflies, no-hackle dry flies, and short bodied nymphs.

Comment: Called the "Hooper Short Shank Dry". Except for the shorter shank length these hooks are identical to Partridge E1A.

Possible Substitutes: Eagle Claw 60; Mustad 94838

Specifications:

SIZES:	10	12	14	16	18
Shank Length (mm)	11	8	7	6	5
Gape (mm)	6	5	4	4	3
Weight (grams)	48	31	26	18	12
Wire Diameter (mm)	.56	.51	46	.41	.36
Bend Resistance (oz.)	24	22	19	18	16

PARTRIDGE

G3A

Wire:	Heavyweight
Shape:	Forged sproat
Eye:	Ball, turned down
Length:	Standard
Finish:	Bronze
Sizes:	8 to 16

Common Uses: Wet flies and nymphs

Possible Substitutes: Eagle Claw 57; Kamasan B-170; Mustad 3906; VMC 8527

Specifications:

SIZES:	8	10	12	14	16
Shank Length (mm)	11	10	7	6	5.5
Gape (mm)	6.5	5.5	5	4.5	3.5
Weight (grams)	95	70	49	32	20
Wire Diameter (mm)	.74	.66	.61	.56	.51
Bend Resistance (oz.)	70	56	44	39	32

H1A

Wire:	2X fine
Shape:	Forged, Captain Hamilton
Eye:	Ball, turned down
Length:	2 1/2X long
Finish:	Bronze
Sizes:	6 to 16

Common Uses: Longer nymphs, lightweight bucktails, grasshoppers, and some larger mayfly dry flies.

Possible Substitutes: Eagle Claw 63; Kamasan B-800; Mustad 94831; Tiemco 5263; VMC 9283

Specifications:

SIZES:	6	8	10	12	14	16
Shank Length (mm)	22	18	15	13	12	9
Gape (mm)	8	6.5	6	5.5	5	4
Weight (grams)	135	120	85	50	49	27
Wire Diameter (mm)	.74	.66	.61	.54	.54	.46
Bend Resistance (oz.)	52	56	52	38	32	24

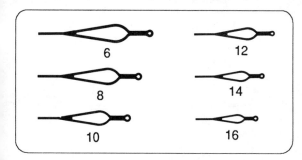

H3ST

Wire:	Heavyweight
Shape:	Forged salmon
Eye:	Straight looped
Length:	6X long
Finish:	Bronze
Sizes:	6 to 16

Common Uses: Flat bodied nymph imitations, particularly stonefly and dragonfly patterns.

Comment: The double shank is brazed into a solid unit, and light serrations on the shank help prevent thread slippage.

Possible Substitutes: None

Specifications:

SIZES:	6	8	10	12	14	16
Shank Length (mm)	23	20	18	16	13	11
Gape (mm)	8.5	7	6	5.5	5	4.5
Weight (grams)	290	220	170	130	85	65
Wire Diameter (mm)	.81	.74	.66	.61	.56	.51
Bend Resistance (oz.)	78	64	52	42	37	28

K1A

Wire:	4X fine
Shape:	Captain Hamilton, offset
Eye:	Ball, turned down
Length:	Standard
Finish:	Bronze
Sizes:	24, 26, 28

P A R T R I D G E

Common Uses: Tiny mayfly and midge dry flies; also midge pupa.

Comment: Called the "Marinaro Midge Hook", it was designed and named for the late Vince Marinaro, author of *A Modern Dry Fly Code* and *In The Ring Of The Rise*.

Possible Substitutes: Mustad 94840 or 94859

Specifications:

SIZES:	24	26	28
Shank Length (mm)	3.5	3	2.5
Gape (mm)	2.1	1.8	1.5
Weight (grams)	5	4	3
Wire Diameter (mm)	.31	.31	.28
Bend Resistance (oz.)	10	10	8

K2B

Wire: Standard
Shape: Forged, special
Eye: Ball, turned up
Finish: Bronze
Sizes: 10 to 16

Common Uses: Caddis pupa and larva, shrimp and grub patterns, also for "upside down" flies.

Comment: Length measurements were not taken since flies are usualy tied well into the bend of the hook.

Possible Substitutes: Mustad 37160

Specifications:

SIZES:	10	12	14	16
Shank Length (mm)	n/a	n/a	n/a	n/a
Gape (mm)	6.5	6	5	4.5
Weight (grams)	72	55	41	32
Wire Diameter (mm)	.66	.61	.56	.51
Bend Resistance (oz.)	48	40	33	22

K3A

Wire: 4X fine
Shape: Forged modified sproat
Eye: Ball, turned down
Length: 2X long
Finish: Bronze
Sizes: 12 to 18

Common Uses: Mayfly and caddisfly dry flies.
Comment: Also known as the "Swedish Dry Fly Hook" originaly designed in Sweden for upright wing mayfly patterns, this hook was popularized for caddisfly dries in Gary LaFontaine's book *Caddisflies.*
Possible Substitutes: None.

Specifications:

SIZES:	12	14	16	18
Shank Length (mm)	14	12	10	8
Gape (mm)	5	4.5	4	3.5
Weight (grams)	49	37	26	20
Wire Diameter (mm)	.51	.46	.41	.41
Bend Resistance (oz.)	24	21	16	20

PARTRIDGE

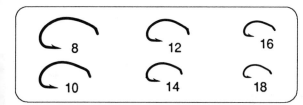

K4A

Wire:	2X fine
Shape:	Special, offset
Eye:	Ball, turned down
Finish:	Bronze
Sizes:	8 to 18

Common Uses: Small grub and shrimp imitations, plus other specialized flies that require an extra wide gape.

Comment: This hook is also known as the "John Veniard Grub/Shrimp" hook. The full curved shank precludes shank length measurements.

Possible Substitutes: Tiemco TMC 2487

Specifications:

SIZES:	8	10	12	14	16	18
Shank Length (mm)	n/a	n/a	n/a	n/a	n/a	n/a
Gape (mm)	8	7	6	4.5	4	3
Weight (grams)	76	60	41	31	20	13
Wire Diameter (mm)	.66	.61	.56	.51	.46	.41
Bend Resistance (oz.)	42	35	32	32	23	24

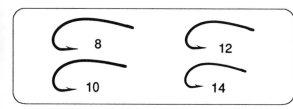

K12ST

Shape:	Special, forged
Eye:	Straight, ball
Length:	3X long
Finish:	Black
Sizes:	8 to 14

Common Uses: Caddis larvae and pupae, shrimp, dragon fly nymphs, and larger soft hackled wet flies.

Comment: Sometimes referred to as the "Longshank Sedge/Caddis Hook". A size #16 will soon be offered.

Possible Substitutes: No hooks are exactly like this design, however the Mustad 37160 might serve as a substitute.

Specifications:

SIZES:	8	10	12	14
Shank Length (mm)	n/a	n/a	n/a	n/a
Gape (mm)	7.5	7	6.5	5.5
Weight (grams)	110	91	74	48
Wire Diameter (mm)	.70	.66	.61	.56
Bend Resistance (oz.)	60	46	38	32

PARTRIDGE

L2A

Wire: 2X fine
Shape: Forged, Captain Hamilton
Eye: Ball, turned down
Length: Standard
Finish: Bronze
Sizes: 8 to 18

Common Uses: Standard dry flies or lightwire wet flies and nymphs.
Comment: This hook is noted for it's short point and small barb. The L3A and L4A models are identical but made with a lighter wire.
Possible Substitutes: Eagle Claw 59; Kamasan B-400; Mustad 94840; VMC 9280

Specifications:

SIZES:	8	10	12	14	16	18
Shank Length (mm)	14	11	9	8	7	5.5
Gape (mm)	6	6	5.5	4.5	4	3.5
Weight (grams)	83	60	43	32	21	15
Wire Diameter (mm)	.66	.61	.56	.51	.46	.41
Bend Resistance (oz.)	46	36	31	24	21	16

L3A

Wire: 4X fine
Shape: Forged, Captain Hamilton
Eye: Ball, turned down
Length: Standard
Finish: Bronze
Sizes: 8 to 22

Common Uses: Standard and sparsely dressed dry flies of all kinds.

Comment: Identical to the L2A but made of a lighter wire. See also L3AY.

Possible Substitutes: Mustad 94833; Tiemco TMC100; VMC 9288

Specifications:

SIZES:	8	10	12	14	16	18	20	22
Shank Length (mm)	13	10	9	8	7	6	5.5	5
Gape (mm)	7	6	5	4.5	4	3.5	3	2.5
Weight (grams)	66	50	35	25	18	12	8	5
Wire Diameter (mm)	.61	.56	.51	.46	.41	.36	.33	.31
Bend Resistance (oz.)	27	24	21	16	22	14	12	6

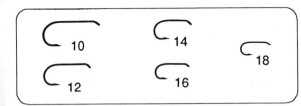

L3AY

Wire: 4X fine
Shape: Forged, Captain Hamilton
Eye: Ball, turned down
Length: Standard
Finish: Bronze
Sizes: 10 to 18

Common Uses: Barbless standard and sparsely dressed dry flies of all kinds.

Comment: Identical to the L3A but barbless.

Possible Substitutes: Eagle Claw 61; Mustad 94845.

Specifications:

SIZES:	10	12	14	16	18
Shank Length (mm)	10	9	8	7	6
Gape (mm)	6	5	4.5	4	3.5
Weight (grams)	50	35	25	18	12
Wire Diameter (mm)	.56	.51	.46	.41	.36
Bend Resistance (oz.)	24	21	16	22	14

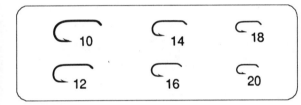

L4A

Wire: 6X fine
Shape: Forged, Captain Hamilton
Eye: Ball, turned down
Length: Standard
Finish: Bronze
Sizes: 10 to 20

Common Uses: No hackle or sparsely dressed dry flies; also floating nymphs.
Comment: This is the lightest weight of the "L" series of hooks; see also L2A and L3A.
Possible Substitutes: Tiemco TMC 5230; Mustad 94833

Specifications:

SIZES:	10	12	14	16	18	20
Shank Length (mm)	10	9	7.5	6.5	5.5	5
Gape (mm)	6	5.5	5	4	3.3	2.8
Weight (grams)	41	30	22	14	10	6
Wire Diameter (mm)	.51	.46	.41	.36	.33	.31
Bend Resistance (oz.)	16	15	13	10	8	7

P
A
R
T
R
I
D
G
E

M

Wire: 2X heavy
Shape: Forged salmon
Eye: Looped, tapered, turned up
Length: Standard
Finish: Black
Sizes: 4/0 to 1/0 and 1 to 10

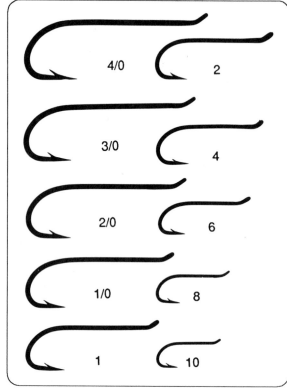

Common Uses: Atlantic Salmon wet flies. Also steelhead wet flies and sinking bass streamers.

Comment: This hook is also occasionally used for trout and bass flies when extra strength is desired.

Possible Substitutes: Mustad 36890; Tiemco TMC 7999

Specifications:

SIZES:	4/0	3/0	2/0	1/0
Shank Length (mm)	32	28	27	25
Gape (mm)	14	14	13	12
Weight (grams)	1020	800	690	590
Wire Diameter (mm)	1.50	1.40	1.32	1.27
Bend Resistance (oz.)	288	272	224	208

Specifications:

SIZES:	1	2	4	6	8	10
Shank Length (mm)	21	18	16	14	12	11
Gape (mm)	11	10	9	8	7	6
Weight (grams)	440	360	275	195	125	90
Wire Diameter (mm)	1.14	1.07	1.02	.94	.84	.76
Bend Resistance (oz.)	192	112	132	124	84	68

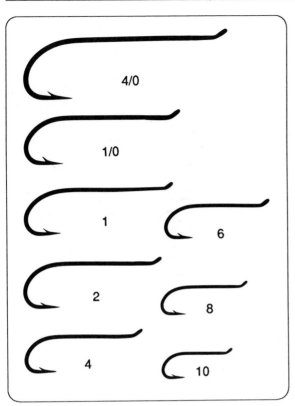

Wire:	1X heavy
Shape:	Forged "low water"
Eye:	Looped, tapered, turned up
Length:	2X long
Finish:	Black
Sizes:	4/0, 1/0 and 1 to 10

Common Uses: Atlantic Salmon flies, both low-water and standard wets.

Comment: Often referred to as the "Partridge Low-Water Salmon Hook", many fly tyers prefer its graceful lines for most of their salmon flies.

Possible Substitutes: Mustad 90240; Kamasan B-180

Specifications:

SIZES:	4/0	1/0
Shank Length (mm)	38	29
Gape (mm)	14	11
Weight (grams)	840	510
Wire Diameter (mm)	1.32	1.14
Bend Resistance (oz.)	176	192

Specifications:

SIZES:	1	2	4	6	8	10
Shank Length (mm)	27	26	22	19	16	13
Gape (mm)	11	10	9	8	7	6
Weight (grams)	410	350	250	190	120	90
Wire Diameter (mm)	1.07	1.02	.94	.84	.76	.69
Bend Resistance (oz.)	112	128	108	92	76	64

P

Wire: 2X heavy
Shape: Salmon
Eye: Looped, turned up
Length: Standard
Finish: Black
Sizes: 2 to 10

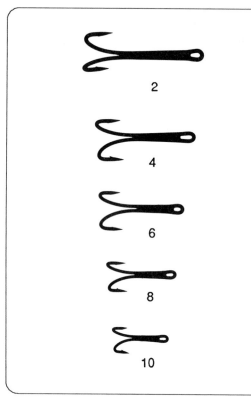

Common Uses: Atlantic Salmon wet flies.

Comment: This is the double version of the Partridge Code M single salmon hook. It is used fo both its added weight as well as stability in the water, and increased holding power.

Possible Substitutes: Mustad 3582C

Specifications:

SIZES:	2	4	6	8	10
Shank Length (mm)	21	17	14	12	10
Gape (mm)	10	9	8	7	6
Weight (grams)	771	550	395	255	165
Wire Diameter (mm)	1.07	1.02	.94	.84	.76
Bend Resistance (oz.)	272	248	192	164	144

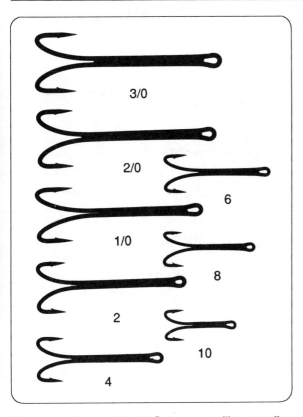

Wire:	1X heavy
Shape:	Forged, low water
Eye:	Looped, turned up
Length:	2X long (salmon scale)
Finish:	Black
Sizes:	3/0, 2/0, 1/0, and 2 to 10

Common Uses: Atlantic Salmon wet flies, steelhead wet flies, and sinking bass flies.

Comment: This is the double version of the Partridge Code N single low water salmon hook.

Possible Substitutes: Mustad 3582F

Specifications:

SIZES:	3/0	2/0	1/0
Shank Length (mm)	38	34	33
Gape (mm)	13	13	12
Weight (grams)	1580	1385	1130
Wire Diameter (mm)	1.27	1.14	1.14
Bend Resistance (oz.)	320	288	336

Specifications:

SIZES:	2	4	6	8	10
Shank Length (mm)	28	24	21	18	14
Gape (mm)	11	10	8	6.5	5.5
Weight (grams)	775	545	385	275	185
Wire Diameter (mm)	1.02	.94	.84	.76	.69
Bend Resistance (oz.)	224	200	184	144	120

01

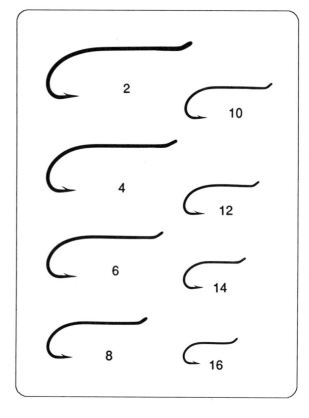

Wire:	Standard
Shape:	Forged Wilson
Eye:	Looped, tapered, turned up
Length:	6X long (salmon scale)
Finish:	Black
Sizes:	2 to 16

Common Uses: Atlantic Salmon dry flies, steelhead dry flies, low- water style salmon, steelhead, and sea trout flies.

Comment: Known as the "Wilson Hook", based on the shape of the bend, and recognized for it's graceful lines.

Possible Substitutes: Mustad 9049

Specifications:

SIZES:	2	4	6	8
Shank Length (mm)	25	23	21	18
Gape (mm)	11	11	10	9
Weight (grams)	380	290	210	150
Wire Diameter (mm)	1.02	.94	.84	.76
Bend Resistance (oz.)	144	104	88	56

Specifications:

SIZES:	10	12	14	16
Shank Length (mm)	15	12	11	10
Gape (mm)	7.5	6.5	6	5.5
Weight (grams)	110	87	64	44
Wire Diameter (mm)	.69	.64	.58	.53
Bend Resistance (oz.)	48	48	44	40

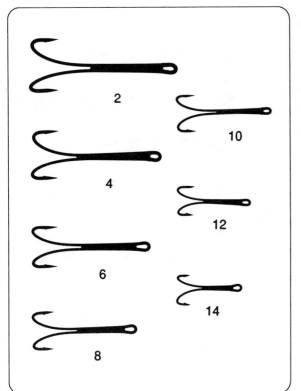

Wire: Standard
Shape: Forged Wilson
Eye: Looped, turned up
Length: 6X long (salmon scale)
Finish: Black
Sizes: 2 to 14

Common Uses: Low -water style salmon, steelhead, and sea trout flies.

Comment: This is the double version of the "Wilson Hook", based on the shape of the bend, and recognized for it's graceful lines.

Possible Substitutes: Mustad 3582F

Specifications:

SIZES:	2	4	6	8
Shank Length (mm)	26	25	21	20
Gape (mm)	11	10	9.5	8
Weight (grams)	780	600	420	340
Wire Diameter (mm)	1.02	.94	84	.76
Bend Resistance (oz.)	192	160	144	128

Specifications:

SIZES:	10	12	14
Shank Length (mm)	18	13	11
Gape (mm)	7	6.5	6.5
Weight (grams)	230	170	120
Wire Diameter (mm)	.69	.64	.58
Bend Resistance (oz.)	116	108	72

CUSTOM

Wire: Standard
Shape: Spey
Eye: Looped, tapered, turned up
Finish: Black, bronze, blued, gold, and silver
Sizes: 1 1/2, 3, 5, 7

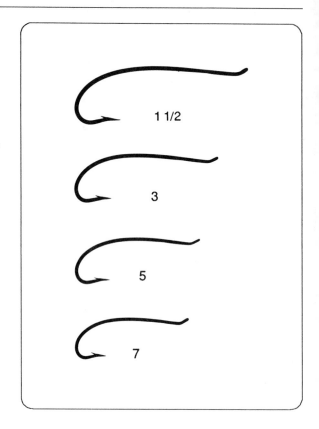

Common Uses: Spey style Atlantic Salmon and steelhead wet flies. This is also a beautiful hook on which to tie flies for display purposes.

Comment: This is a custom hook being produced for, and available through, Alec Jackson at "The Yorkshire Flyfisher", P.O. Box 386, Kenmore, WA 98028

Possible Substitutes: None

Specifications:

SIZES:	1 1/2	3	5	7
Shank Length (mm)	n/a	n/a	n/a	n/a
Gape (mm)	13	10	9	8
Weight (grams)	480	340	260	215
Wire Diameter (mm)	1.09	.99	.91	.79
Bend Resistance (oz.)	152	136	128	108

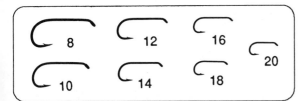

TMC 100

Shape:	Round
Eye:	Ball, turned down
Finish:	Bronze
Sizes:	8 to 20

Common Uses: Standard dry flies and floating nymphs.

Possible Substitutes: Eagle Claw 59; Mustad 94833; Partridge L3A; Kamasan B-400

Specifications:

SIZES:	8	10	12	14	16	18	20
Shank Length (mm)	11	10	9	8	7.5	6	5
Gape (mm)	6	5.5	5	4.5	4	3.5	3
Weight (grams)	72	48	32	23	15	11	10
Wire Diameter (mm)	.63	.57	.51	.45	.41	.37	.36
Bend Resistance (oz.)	34	26	22	17	12	13	14

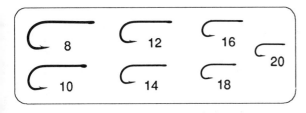

TMC 101

Shape:	Round
Eye:	Ball, straight
Finish:	Bronze
Sizes:	8 to 20

Common Uses: Dry flies and floating nymphs.

Comment: This hook is essentially identical to Tiemco model TMC100 except that the eye is straight.

Possible Substitutes: None, as this is the only straight eye dry fly hook being offered.

Specifications:

SIZES:	8	10	12	14	16	18	20
Shank Length (mm)	12	11	9	8	7	6	5
Gape (mm)	6	5.5	5	4.5	4	3.5	3
Weight (grams)	72	48	32	23	15	11	8
Wire Diameter (mm)	.63	.57	.51	.45	.41	.38	.36
Bend Resistance (oz.)	30	26	22	19	16	14	13

TIEMCO

TMC 102

Shape: Round
Eye: Ball, turned down
Finish: Bronze
Sizes: 11, 13, 15, 17

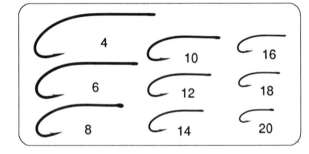

Common Uses: Dry flies and floating nymphs.
Comment: This range is designed to fit between the standard (even numbered) sizes in Tiemco's model TMC100.
Possible Substitutes: Due to variations in hook design, other manufacturers have hooks with similar measurements, but they lack the odd-numbered designations.

Specifications:

SIZES:	11	13	15	17
Shank Length (mm)	9	8	7	6
Gape (mm)	5.5	5	4.5	4
Weight (grams)	41	27	21	12
Wire Diameter (mm)	.53	.48	.41	.38
Bend Resistance (oz.)	28	17	13	16

TMC 200

Shape: Special
Eye: Ball, straight
Finish: Bronze
Sizes: 4 to 20

Common Uses: Nymphs
Comment: The design of this hook results in a very graceful appearing nymph imitation.
Possible Substitutes: No other hooks have a bend comparable to this model.

Specifications:

SIZE:	4	6	8	10	12	14	16	18	20
Shank Length (mm)	n/a	n/a	n/a	n/a	n/a	n/a	n/a	n/a	n/a
Gape (mm)	8	7	6	5	4.5	4	3.5	3	2.5
Weight (grams)	147	126	97	60	43	31	21	14	11
Wire Diameter (mm)	.69	.71	.66	.58	.56	.48	.43	.41	.38
Bend Resistance (oz.)	34	48	34	32	27	20	19	18	15

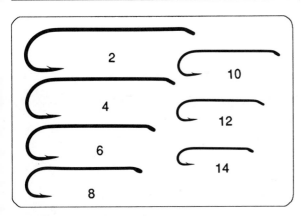

TMC 300

Shape:	Round
Eye:	Ball, turned down
Finish:	Bronze
Sizes:	2 to 14

Common Uses: Streamers, bucktails and stonefly nymphs.
Possible Substitutes: Mustad 79580; Kamasan B-800; Eagle Claw 281; VMC 9283

Specifications:

SIZES:	2	4	6	8	10	12	14
Shank Length (mm)	36	31	26	24	21	18	15
Gape (mm)	10	9	8	7	6	5	4
Weight (grams)	385	285	235	150	96	75	58
Wire Diameter (mm)	.99	.91	.86	.74	63	.61	.58
Bend Resistance (oz.)	96	76	88	60	40	46	45

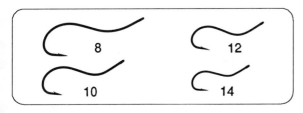

TMC 400T

Shape:	Special
Eye:	Ball, straight
Finish:	Bronze
Sizes:	8 to 14

Common Uses: "Swimming nymphs", particularly larger mayfly nymphs; also leech patterns.

Possible Substitutes: No other hook manufacturer offers this unusual shape.

Specifications:

SIZES:	8	10	12	14
Shank Length (mm)	n/a	n/a	n/a	n/a
Gape (mm)	8.5	7	6	5
Weight (grams)	93	64	44	29
Wire Diameter (mm)	.61	.53	.48	.43
Bend Resistance (oz.)	22	20	14	12

TMC 2302

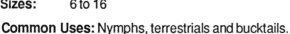

Wire:	Standard
Shape:	Special, forged
Eye:	Ball, straight
Length:	2X long
Finish:	Bronze
Sizes:	6 to 16

Common Uses: Nymphs, terrestrials and bucktails.

Comment: The slight curve of the shank adds a graceful appearance to the finished fly. Shank length has not been measured as the body of the fly may be tied into the bend of the hook. See TMC 2312 for a similar, but lighter wire, hook.

Possible Substitutes: No other hook has this curved shank.

Specifications:

SIZES:	6	8	10	12	14	16
Shank Length (mm)	n/a	n/a	n/a	n/a	n/a	n/a
Gape (mm)	7.5	6.5	5.5	5	4	3.5
Weight (grams)	140	105	68	47	31	22
Wire Diameter (mm)	.79	.69	.64	.56	.48	.43
Bend Resistance (oz.)	64	40	32	34	26	23

TMC 2312

Wire:	1X fine
Shape:	Special, forged
Eye:	Ball, straight
Length:	2X long
Finish:	Bronze
Sizes:	6 to 16

Common Uses: Nymphs, terrestrials and grasshoppers.

Comment: This hook is essentially identical to TMC 2302 except for the wire diameter.

Possible Substitutes: No other hook has this curved shank.

Specifications:

SIZES:	6	8	10	12	14	16
Shank Length (mm)	n/a	n/a	n/a	n/a	n/a	n/a
Gape (mm)	7.5	6.0	5.5	5	4	3.5
Weight (grams)	125	88	58	51	28	17
Wire Diameter (mm)	.71	.64	.58	.51	.46	.41
Bend Resistance (oz.)	50	37	30	25	20	17

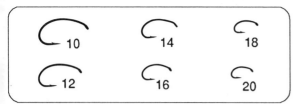

TMC 2487

Wire:	Fine
Shape:	Special, forged, offset
Eye:	Ball, turned down
Length:	2X short
Finish:	Bronze
Sizes:	10 to 20

Common Uses: Floating nymphs, shrimp, and caddis pupae.

Possible Substitutes: Partridge K4A

Specifications:

SIZES:	10	12	14	16	18	20
Shank Length (mm)	n/a	n/a	n/a	n/a	n/a	n/a
Gape (mm)	6.5	5.5	4.5	3.5	3	2.5
Weight (grams)	41	27	21	14	11	9
Wire Diameter (mm)	.50	.46	.43	.38	.36	.36
Bend Resistance (oz.)	21	17	20	16	16	14

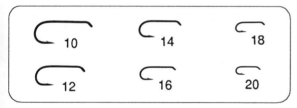

TMC 5210

Wire:	1X fine
Shape:	Modified round
Eye:	Ball, turned down
Finish:	Bronze
Sizes:	10 to 20

Common Uses: Dry flies and floating nymphs

Possible Substitutes: Eagle Claw 59; Kamasan B-400; Mustad 94840; Partridge E1A; VMC 9288

Specifications:

SIZES:	10	12	14	16	18	20
Shank Length (mm)	11	9	8	7	5.5	5
Gape (mm)	5.5	5	4	3	2.5	2
Weight (grams)	47	34	23	14	10	7
Wire Diameter (mm)	.53	.48	.43	.38	.36	.30
Bend Resistance (oz.)	20	18	17	14	14	10

TMC 5230

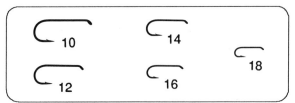

Wire: 3X fine
Shape: Modified round
Eye: Ball, turned down
Finish: Bronze
Sizes: 10 to 18

Common Uses: No hackle and sparsely tied dry flies; also floating nymphs.

Possible Substitutes: Mustad 94833; Partridge L4A; VMC 9288

Specifications:

SIZES:	10	12	14	16	18
Shank Length (mm)	11	9	8	7	6
Gape (mm)	5.5	5	4	3	2.5
Weight (grams)	38	26	17	12	7
Wire Diameter (mm)	.48	.43	.38	.36	.30
Bend Resistance (oz.)	15	14	11	10	8

TMC 5262

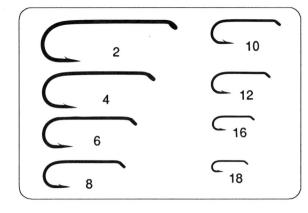

Shape: Forged round
Eye: Ball, turned down
Length: 2X long
Finish: Bronze
Sizes: 2 to 18

Common Uses: Nymphs, streamers, bucktails and muddlers.
Possible Substitutes: Eagle Claw 63; Kamasan B-830; Mustad 9671;
VMC 9279
Specifications:

SIZES:	2	4	6	8	10	12	14	16	18
Shank Length (mm)	28	23	18	15	13	11	9	8	7
Gape (mm)	10	9	7	6.5	6	5	4.5	4.5	3
Weight (grams)	335	235	175	120	77	43	30	24	13
Wire Diameter (mm)	.99	.90	.84	.74	.64	.58	.53	.46	.40
Bend Resistance (oz.)	96	88	80	64	48	42	38	32	30

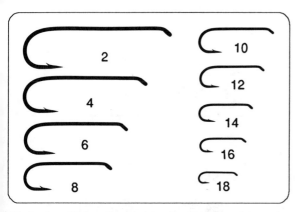

TMC 5263

Shape:	Forged round
Eye:	Ball, turned down
Length:	3X long
Finish:	Bronze
Sizes:	2 to 18

Common Uses: Streamers, bucktails and nymphs.
Possible Substitutes: Eagle Claw 58; Kamasan B-830; Mustad 9672; Partridge H1A; VMC 9279

Specifications:

SIZES:	2	4	6	8	10	12	14	16	18
Shank Length (mm)	29	25	21	17	15	12	11	9	8
Gape (mm)	10	8.5	7.5	7	6	5	4	3.5	3
Weight (grams)	345	250	185	125	81	55	38	26	15
Wire Diameter (mm)	.99	.90	.84	.74	.64	.58	.53	.46	.40
Bend Resistance (oz.)	96	88	80	68	43	34	32	28	27

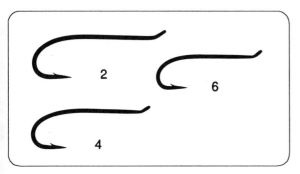

TMC 7999

Wire:	Heavy
Shape:	Forged, salmon
Eye:	Tapered, looped, turned up
Finish:	Black
Sizes:	2 to 6

Common Uses: Steelhead and Atlantic Salmon wet flies.
Comment: Additional sizes are planned in the very near future.
Possible Substitutes: Kamasan B-180; Mustad 36890; Partridge M

Specifications:

SIZES:	2	4	6
Shank Length (mm)	22	19	17
Gape (mm)	10	9	7.5
Weight (grams)	400	295	225
Wire Diameter (mm)	1.14	1.04	.97
Bend Resistance (oz.)	160	144	120

TIEMCO

8410

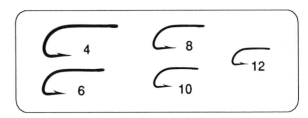

Shape: Forged, "crystal"
Eye: Ball, straight
Finish: Bronze
Sizes: 4 to 12

Common Uses: Saltwater streamers and bass flies.

Comment: Available in Nickel (8410N); Gold (8410G); and Perma Steel (8410PS). Larger sizes may soon become available.

Specifications:

SIZES:	4	6	8	10	12
Shank Length (mm)	11	9	8	6	5
Gape (mm)	7	6	5.5	4.5	4
Weight (grams)	135	88	63	35	26
Wire Diameter (mm)	.81	.71	.58	.50	.48
Bend Resistance (oz.)	80	72	40	32	32

8526

Shape: Sproat
Eye: Forged ball, turned down
Finish: Bronze
Sizes: 8 to 16

Common Uses: Wet flies and nymphs.

Comment: See model 8527 for a similar hook with a longer shank.

Possible Substitutes: Mustad 3399A

Specifications:

SIZE:	8	10	12	14	16
Shank Length (mm)	8	7	6.5	5.5	5
Gape (mm)	6.5	5	4.5	4	3
Weight (grams)	98	68	45	32	19
Wire Diameter (mm)	.74	.66	.58	.53	.43
Bend Resistance (oz.)	64	50	36	32	25

V
M
C

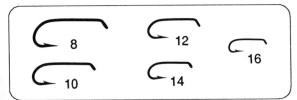

8527

Shape: Sproat
Eye: Forged ball, turned down
Length: X long
Finish: Bronze
Sizes: 8 to 16

Common Uses: Nymphs and small bucktails.

Comment: Same as model 8526 but with a longer shank.

Possible Substitutes: Eagle Claw 57; Mustad 3399A; Partridge G3A

Specifications:

SIZES:	8	10	12	14	16
Shank Length (mm)	12	10	8	7	6
Gape (mm)	6.5	5	4.5	4	3
Weight (grams)	110	80	52	38	22
Wire Diameter (mm)	.74	.66	.58	.53	.43
Bend Resistance (oz.)	68	56	40	32	24

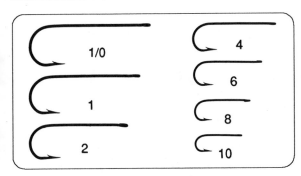

9145

Wire: 3X fine
Shape: Round
Eye: Ball, straight
Finish: Bronze
Sizes: 1/0 to 10

Common Uses: Bass and shad flies
Comment: Also available in Gold (9145G); and Blued (9145B) finishes.
Possible Substitutes: Partridge H1A

Specifications:

SIZES:	1/0	1	2	4	6	8	10
Shank Length (mm)	25	23	20	17	14	11	9
Gape (mm)	10	9	8.5	6.5	6	5	4
Weight (grams)	170	145	125	74	46	35	28
Wire Diameter (mm)	.76	.74	.71	.61	.53	.50	.48
Bend Resistance (oz.)	34	32	28	23	16	20	20

V
M
C

9148

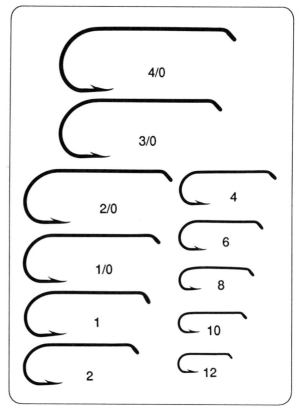

Shape: Round, Aberdeen
Eye: Ball, turned down
Finish: Bronze
Sizes: 4/0 to 12

Common Uses: Lightwire streamers in smaller sizes; bass, shad, and saltwater flies.

Comment: Also available in Nickel (9148N), and Gold (9148G)

Possible Substitutes: Partridge CS11

Specifications:

SIZES:	4/0	3/0	2/0	1/0
Shank Length (mm)	35	32	29	27
Gape (mm)	15.5	14	12.5	11.5
Weight (grams)	550	435	360	295
Wire Diameter (mm)	1.12	.99	.96	.89
Bend Resistance (oz.)	72	60	52	44

Specifications:

SIZES:	1	2	4	6	8	10	12
Shank Length (mm)	25	23	20	17	15	14	11
Gape (mm)	11	10	8	7	5.5	5	4.5
Weight (grams)	240	195	140	105	86	62	45
Wire Diameter (mm)	.86	.81	.76	.69	.66	.61	.56
Bend Resistance (oz.)	42	32	32	30	36	30	25

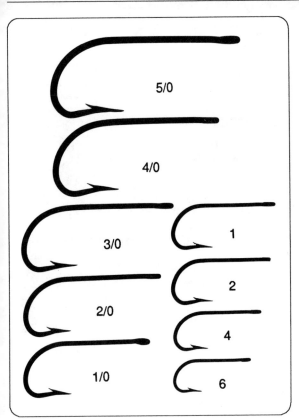

9255

Shape: O'Shaughnessy
Eye: Ball, straight
Length: Long shank
Finish: Bronze
Sizes: 5/0 to 6

Common Uses: Saltwater streamers, bass, and shad flies.

Comment: Also available in Nickel (9255N); Perma Steel (9255PS); and Gold (9255G)

Possible Substitutes: Eagle Claw 254SS or 178; Mustad 34007

Specifications:

SIZES:	5/0	4/0	3/0	2/0	1/0
Shank Length (mm)	31	27	25	24	21
Gape (mm)	18	17	15	13	13
Weight (grams)	1670	1195	820	630	515
Wire Diameter (mm)	1.80	1.60	1.40	1.30	1.20
Bend Resistance (oz.)	288	264	192	184	132

Specifications:

SIZES:	1	2	4	6
Shank Length (mm)	18	18	15	13
Gape (mm)	10	10	9	8
Weight (grams)	290	290	195	135
Wire Diameter (mm)	1.02	1.02	.89	.81
Bend Resistance (oz.)	112	112	96	72

V
M
C

9279

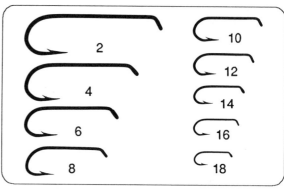

Shape: Forged, modified round
Eye: Forged ball, turned down
Length: 2X long
Finish: Bronze
Sizes: 2 to 18

Common Uses: Streamers, bucktails, muddlers, hairwing and larger dry flies.

Possible Substitutes: Mustad 9671; Partridge D4A; Kamasan B-830; Tiemco TMC 5263; Eagle Claw 63

Specifications:

SIZES:	2	4	6	8	10	12	14	16	18
Shank Length (mm)	27	22	19	15	14	12	10	7	5.5
Gape (mm)	9	8.5	8	7	5.5	5	4	3	2.5
Weight (grams)	345	260	175	120	83	67	41	16	12
Wire Diameter (mm)	1.02	.94	.86	.76	.66	.58	.53	.38	.38
Bend Resistance (oz.)	116	112	88	72	48	40	32	19	17

9280

Wire: Extra fine
Shape: Forged, modified round
Eye: Forged ball, turned down
Finish: Bronze
Sizes: 6 to 20

Common Uses: Standard and hairwing dry flies

Possible Substitutes: Eagle Claw 61; Kamasan B-400; Mustad 7948A; Partridge L2A

Specifications:

SIZES:	6	8	10	12	14	16	18	20
Shank Length (mm)	14	11	10	10	8	6	6	4
Gape (mm)	7	6	5.5	4.5	4	3	2.5	2
Weight (grams)	120	80	69	42	28	16	10	6
Wire Diameter (mm)	.76	.69	.66	.56	.48	.38	.33	.33
Bend Resistance (oz.)	52	48	46	32	23	18	14	18

V
M
C

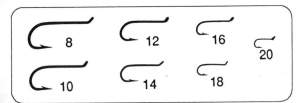

9281

Wire: Extra fine
Shape: Forged, modified round
Eye: Forged ball, turned up
Finish: Bronze
Sizes: 8 to 20

Common Uses: Traditional dry flies and lightweight nymph imitations.

Comment: Essentially the same as 9280 but with an upturned eye.

Possible Substitutes: Mustad 94842; Eagle Claw 159

Specifications:

SIZES:	8	10	12	14	16	18	20
Shank Length (mm)	12	10	9	8	7	6	4
Gape (mm)	6	5.5	4.5	4	3	2.5	2
Weight (grams)	81	68	42	26	15	10	4
Wire Diameter (mm)	.66	.64	.53	.48	.38	.33	.28
Bend Resistance (oz.)	46	42	31	24	16	12	12

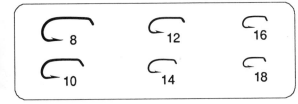

9282

Wire: Extra fine
Shape: Forged, sproat, offset
Eye: Forged, ball, turned down
Finish: Bronze
Sizes: 8 to 18

Common Uses: Dry and wet flies, beetles and ant imitations.
Comment: The offset bend might be an aid to hooking ability in the smaller sizes.
Possible Substitutes: Mustad 7958; Partridge A

Specifications:

SIZES:	8	10	12	14	16	18
Shank Length (mm)	9	7	6	5	4	4
Gape (mm)	6	4	3.5	3	2.5	2
Weight (grams)	68	45	27	16	11	9
Wire Diameter (mm)	.72	.61	.51	.41	.38	.36
Bend Resistance (oz.)	68	54	32	22	20	18

V M C

9283

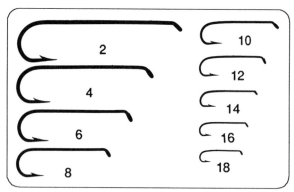

Shape: Forged, round
Eye: Forged ball, turned down
Length: 4X long
Finish: Bronze
Sizes: 2 to 18

Common Uses: Streamers and bucktails, also stonefly nymphs in larger sizes, mayfly nymphs in smaller sizes.
Possible Substitutes: Eagle Claw 58; Kamasan B-800; Mustad 79580; Partridge H1A

Specifications:

SIZES:	2	4	6	8	10	12	14	16	18
Shank Length (mm)	36	29	25	21	16	13	12	10	8
Gape (mm)	10	9	7.5	7	5.5	5	4	3	3
Weight (grams)	390	265	180	125	69	42	30	20	13
Wire Diameter (mm)	1.02	.89	.79	.74	.61	.53	.46	.38	.33
Bend Resistance (oz.)	112	88	68	64	34	20	20	17	14

9288

Wire: 2X fine
Shape: Forged, round
Eye: Forged, ball, turned down
Length: Short
Finish: Bronze
Sizes: 6 to 20

Common Uses: Traditional dry flies and variants

Possible Substitutes: Eagle Claw 59; Mustad 94833; Partridge L3A; Tiemco TMC 5230

Specifications:

SIZES:	6	8	10	12	14	16	18	20
Shank Length (mm)	16	12	10	8	6	5	4	4
Gape (mm)	7	6	5	4.5	3.5	3	2.5	2
Weight (grams)	100	72	45	28	16	9	7	6
Wire Diameter (mm)	.71	.64	.53	.51	.46	.30	.28	.27
Bend Resistance (oz.)	56	40	30	22	20	10	8	7

V
M
C

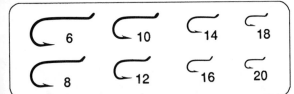

9289

Wire: 2X fine
Shape: Forged, round
Eye: Forged, ball, turned up
Length: Short
Finish: Bronze
Sizes: 6 to 20

Common Uses: Traditional dry flies and light wire nymphs.

Possible Substitutes: Eagle Claw 159; Mustad 94842

Specifications:

SIZES:	6	8	10	12	14	16	18	20
Shank Length (mm)	12	10	8	7	6	4.5	4	4
Gape (mm)	6.5	6	5	4.5	4	3	2.5	2
Weight (grams)	77	58	41	28	15	8	7	5
Wire Diameter (mm)	.64	.58	.53	.48	.41	.30	.28	.25
Bend Resistance (oz.)	35	30	29	26	14	9	8	8

V
M
C